UNDERSTANDING
FOREIGN
EXCHANGE

BASICS
OPERATIONS
MANAGEMENT

Nadir Khan
MBA, DAIBP, DIBF,
Diploma in Accountancy (ACCA)

©Copy Rights 2022, reserved with the author.
The characters and events portrayed in this book are fictitious. Any similarity to real persons, living or dead is co-incidental and not intended by the author.
No part of this book may be reproduced, or stored in a retrieval system, or transmitted in any form or by any means, electronic, mechanical, photocopying, recording, or otherwise, without express written permission of the publisher.
ISBN: 9798371121387

DEDICATED TO IBADALLAH

Table of Contents

PREFACE

CHAPTER ONE

FOREIGN EXCHANGE 1
INTRODUCTION 1
INTERESTED PARTIES 2
TRADERS 3
INVESTORS 4
SPECULATORS 5
HEDGING 5
HISTORY AT A GLANCE 6
FOREIGN EXCHANGE MARKETS 10
FOREIGN EXCHANGE TRADING CENTRES 11
FOREIGN EXCHANGE MARKET- PARTICIPANTS 12
COMMERCIAL BANKS 13
CENTRAL BANKS 14
ADVISORY SERVICES 15
BROKERAGE HOUSES 15

CHAPTER TWO

FOREIGN EXCHANGE BASICS 17
SPOT EXCHANGE RATES 17
DUALITY OF RATES- (BID & OFFER) 20
EXCHANGE RATE QUOTATION CONVENTIONS 21
DIRECT / EUROPEAN QUOTATION 22
INDIRECT /AMERICAN TERMS QUOTATION 23
CROSS RATES 25
OPPOSITE RULE METHOD 26
CHAIN EQUATION METHOD 28
FORWARD RATES 31
FORWARD RATE QUOTATION- TWO WAY 35
FORWARD WITH FIXED AND OPTIONAL DATES 40
FACTORS AFFECTING FORWARD POINTS 41
DETERMINANTS OF FX RATES 42
PURCHASING POWER PARITY (INFLATION) 43
BALANCE OF PAYMENTS 46
INTEREST RATES 46
POLITICAL AND PSYCHOLOGICAL 48
TECHNICAL 48

CHAPTER THREE

FOREIGN EXCHANGE INSTRUMENTS 50
SPOT FX TRANSACTIONS 50
FX RETAIL TRANSACTIONS 50
FX WHOLESALE TRANSACTIONS 51

FOREIGN EXCHANGE DEAL 52
FORWARD CONTRACTs 56
FOREIGN EXCHANGE SWAP 61
SPOT AGAINST FORWARD SWAP 62
FORWARD AGAINST FORWARD SWAP 62
SHORT PERIOD / BROKEN PERIOD SWAP 62
FORWARD SWAP POINT'S QUOTATION 62
USERS OF SWAP 64

CHAPTER FOUR

FOREIGN EXCHANGE DERIVATIVES 65
CURRENCY SWAPS 65
CURRENCY FUTURES 67
FORWARD CONTRACTS VS FUTURE CONTRACTS 67
CURRENCY FUTURE OPERATION 70
INITIAL MARGINAL DEPOSIT 70
LEVERAGING OR GEARING 71
VARIATION MARGIN 72
LIQUIDATION 72
CURRENCY OPTION 73
TYPES OF CURRENCY OPTIONS 74
CALL OPTIONS 74
PUT OPTIONS 75
FORMS OF CURRENCY OPTIONS 75
EXCHANGE TRADED OPTIONS 77
PARTICIPANTS OF THE OPTIONS MARKET 80

CHAPTER FIVE

FOREIGN EXCHANGE MANAGEMENT 82
RISKS INVOLVED IN FOREIGN EXCHANGE 83
EXCHANGE RATE RISK 83
INTEREST RATE RISK 84
CREDIT RISK 84
SETTLEMENT RISK 85
POLITICAL AND LEGAL RISK 85
MANAGING THE RISKS 86
EXCHANGE RATE RISK & INTEREST RATE RISK 86
CASH MANAGEMENT 88
GAP ANALYSIS 88
COVERAGE OF POLITICAL AND LEGAL RISK 90
FX TERMINOLOGIES I
REFERENCES VII

PREFACE

Over the period of last five decades very deep, exciting and irreversible development has occurred in the world of finance and financial institutions. The replacement of fixed exchange rate with flexible exchange rate, the use of sophisticated technologies, the increase in number and use of financial institutions, the ease of transfer of capital and investments across frontiers, the globalization of economies have not only been challenging but also create new opportunities for organizations, firms and individuals. Acquisition of new skills and knowledge has never been as direly felt as these are sought after today. The traders, managers, and foreign exchange professionals need to equip themselves with know-how of foreign exchange for the best performance in their professional roles.

"Understanding Foreign Exchange" is an excellent resource for all those seeking a comprehensive understanding of the nitty-gritty of foreign exchange, foreign market and its related topics. This book has been divided into five chapters the first of which covers various important aspects of foreign exchange. Chapter 2 contains foreign exchange rates including method of identification of exchange rates, its expression and quotation conventions, calculation. These foundational concepts are explained with the help of illustrative examples, which greatly enhance the reader's comprehension. The author provides insights into market participants, the structure of the market, and the factors that influence exchange rates. This comprehensive coverage ensures that the reader develop a lucid understanding as to how the foreign exchange market operates. Chapter 3 delves into the foreign exchange instruments. The author explains these instruments in a detailed yet accessible manner, highlighting their features, uses, and the markets where they are traded. Chapter 4 relates to forex derivatives. This section is valuable for traders, investors, and anyone interested in leveraging these instruments for risk management or speculative purposes. The last chapter 5 is dedicated to risk management in foreign exchange. The author explores different techniques and strategies to mitigate foreign exchange risk, providing practical insight to the traders, investors, and international bankers regarding its application in their day to day operations. This emphasis on risk management adds immense value to the overall content of the book. A glossary of terms used in foreign exchange business is given in the last section of the book.

Nadir Khan
December 2022

Chapter one

FOREIGN EXCHANGE

Introduction

Foreign Exchange (FX) emanates from International Trade and/or International finance. Had there been no international trade or international finance, there would have been definitely no subject in the name of "Foreign Exchange". But since no country is self sufficient in all its economic resources and requirements and there is no single currency in the world due to individual economic performance and national wealth, it has made the subject not only inevitable but also rendered it complexities. As observed by a French Economist **_Gaeten Pirou_** that Foreign Exchange deals spring from the "coexistence between the internationalism of trade and the nationalism of currencies".

Days of barter trade, coins, and gold are gone. We live in the age of paper money, plastic money and electronic coins. Give and take transactions, debit and credit is done through what is called money or currency. My currency is my local and your currency is your local. But my currency is foreign currency for you and vice versa. Therefore it is traded like commodity in the world financial markets.

Foreign exchange is the trading of one currency in exchange for another. Oxford Dictionary defines it as "the money of another country than that of your own". **_Dr Paul Einzing_** in his book "Text Book of Foreign Exchange" defines foreign exchange as "system of converting one national currency into another and of transferring the ownership of money from one country to another". One party buys a specific currency from counterparty in exchange for another currency. The relative amount of the two currencies is determined by the exchange rate between the two currencies. Foreign exchange transaction can be executed in variable amounts on & for different dates and denominations. There is no standardized contract size or dates. The date and amount are determined by the requirements of the contracting parties.

Foreign Exchange markets have become more important due to globalization as the world economies have become more integrated. Foreign exchange rates have begun to affect ever larger segment of the economy. Exchange rates are clearly dependent in some ways on the monetary policies of the major countries. Unstable exchange rates hinder International trade. Costly currency is detrimental to export of a country whereas cheaper currency contributes to inflation and makes the imports dearer in terms of home currency. International trade and finance has direct impact on the exchange rates of currencies. Variety of transactions has given birth to variety of exchange rates. Operation in the international market has increased the understanding of exchange rates mechanism for the benefit of all attached to it. Various rates used in Foreign Exchange Market and the mechanism of their calculation and application are explained through the book in your hands.

INTERESTED PARTIES

Individuals, companies and firms, trade domestically & internationally. Those involved in local trading transact in local currency. But those traders and manufacturers that undertake international business transactions also undertake foreign exchange transactions i.e. to sell, buy, lend and/or borrow across international frontiers, where local currency of the buyer or borrower is a foreign currency to the seller or lender across the border. Since each country has its own currency which is different and foreign to the other country, there is obviously need for money in one currency to be converted to another currency for cross border trading and other numerous transactions.

TRADERS

F.C PURCHASERS

Importers: Importers import raw material, Plant & Machinery, technologies, services like insurance, technical fees etc; for which they need foreign exchange for payment to the exporters and service providers.

Travelers: Travelers and visitors to foreign countries need foreign exchange (currency of the visiting country) for meeting their expenses. They need to purchase the currency of the visiting country.

Services: Foreign Airlines, shipping companies and insurance companies for using cross border services, need foreign exchange to meet their expenses.

Exporters: Exporters need to purchase foreign exchange for payment of commission to indenters and payment of advertising & marketing expenses etc.

Profits: Foreign companies operating locally need to purchase foreign currency/ exchange to repatriate profit as per terms of the business.

Subscriptions: Membership fee, purchase of books and news papers, professional fees, publication fees, education fees etc.

Capital: Transfer of capital/ investment subject to exchange control regulations.

F.C SELLERS

Exporters: Exporters receive proceeds in foreign currency. On receipt of proceeds of goods and /or services in foreign currency, the exporter sells the proceeds against local currency or surrender to the central bank as per regulation in force. In case an exporter demands payment in his own (domestic) currency, the foreign buyer must obtain the home currency of exporter to make the payment from the market or central bank as the case may be.

Expatriates: Beneficiaries of home remittances convert foreign currency into local currency for consumption.

Services: Local Airlines, shipping companies and insurance companies for using cross border services, need foreign exchange to meet their expenses.

Agents: Services like agents, advertising and marketing are provided to foreign companies. Fees and commission received in foreign currency are surrendered against local currency.

Some international trades are transacted in a foreign currency to both the buyer and seller e.g. trading in oil and defense equipment are settled in US$.

INVESTORS

Project finance and international investments also give rise to cross border transactions, for which foreign currency has to be purchased or borrowed. They need to convert some of the money they receive into currency in which they pay for goods. For example, Japanese investors wishing to buy US Treasury bonds/bills will need to buy US dollars in exchange for JPY to make their purchases of US bond or treasury bills. M/S Daewoo (Korean), if undertakes to construct Motorway in Pakistan has to convert into PKRs their money for payment to the locals for goods & service provided and also reconvert into foreign currency the earning from the contract to be taken back into their accounts maintained in their home country. Similarly, a company that buys an asset in a foreign country has to pay for it in the local currency and so will need to convert its home currency into the local foreign currency. Likewise the Oil Exploration firms/companies, they payout money in one currency and receive money in another currency.

SPECULATORS

Traders in currencies can make profits in currency sale purchase. Buy a currency at one rate in a market or from a customer and selling it in another market or to other customer at a more favorable rate. The Foreign exchange rates between two currencies vary in line with relative supply and demand for the two currencies. The more buyers (individuals or companies etc.) that want to purchase a currency will be expensive and the less people or legal entities want to sell a currency, it will be cheap. This activity referred to as speculative trading, makeup by far the largest proportion of trading in the Foreign exchange market.

HEDGING

Companies holding assets in foreign countries like factories, contracts, projects are exposed to the risk of fluctuation in value of those assets in their home currency due to fluctuation in Foreign exchange rates between the two relevant currencies. Companies can eliminate these risks of potential profits and value of assets by hedging as executing a Foreign exchange transaction which will exactly offset the loss of foreign asset caused by fluctuation in the Foreign exchange rates.

Growth in foreign exchange trading over recent years has been stimulated by the liberalization of international trade (the reduction in trade barriers i.e. duties & taxes) and the trend towards the removal of exchange controls.

Many of the leading trading nations now permit the free movement of capital so that firms and individuals can buy, sell, borrow and lend foreign currencies without restrictions. However, the abolition of restrictions on foreign trade and investments is yet to materialize.

HISTORY AT A GLANCE

Foreign Exchange rate basically started to make possible the exchange of currencies for making the international trade possible among the nations sans Barter trade. Local trade was possible with local currencies but foreign trade entailed exchange rates for the conversion of one currency into other. Actually this is the reason behind the evolution of Foreign exchange over time to facilitate the countries to settle their international payments.

Historically world monetary exchange took different forms and practiced various systems over the period of time. Centuries ago barter (exchange of goods and services) functioned as a method of payment. Progress was made by the use of coins bearing the decree of the state authority, merchant or a Banker. The use of metal coins gradually became common place in international trade. However with increase of coins in circulation and its acceptance for value as a medium of exchange, professional money changer in the ancient Middle East started to exchange certain coins on the basis of coins themselves. That was the start of Foreign Exchange trading in crude form.

Phenomenal change in political atmosphere and conditions of countries on world map, like collapse of Roman Empire, the progress in use of coins was taken away from the business trading. It was after eleven century when foreign exchange returned to the international trade. The merchant while meeting the increased demand in international trade evolved banking thereby introducing bill of exchange (an unconditional order in writing directing the addressee to pay a specified sum to a third party). This order (bill of exchange) became transferable by the payee and brought about an impetus to foreign Exchange dealings among the nations. Despite of the progress in the Foreign Markets, there were still problems as the religious leaders/authorities and some governments eyed such dealings and never approved it. Hazardous communication and perilous travel posed another obstacle to trade.

A remarkable step was taken for doing away with the communication hurdles during late 1800 when North America and Europe were connected by laying down a cable across the Atlantic. It provided the basis for today's global financial markets. For almost three and half decades (1880 to 1914) until the start of World War I, payment between countries was made under Gold Standard. Gold standard was defined by **G. Thomas** as "a monetary system in which the value of each basic unit of country's currency is fixed in terms of gold". This system was practiced through one of the three forms in different jurisdictions;

Gold Currency Standard; The system characterized by the circulation of Gold coins. There was free coinage of gold and accepted as a legal tender. The main advantages of Gold Standard were that domestically it acted as powerful check on over issue of currency and internationally it provided stability to exchange between countries in which Gold standard was effectively implemented with public confidence.

Gold Bullion Standard; with passage of time and experience it was found later more convenient to issue Bank notes at absolute parity with Gold and convertible in gold. It conferred on the holder the right to demand Gold Bullion from the central Bank at any time and in unlimited quantity.

Gold Exchange Standard; The Standard was characterized by fixed exchange rates in relation to Gold. The amount of Gold required for backing the paper money. Gold coins conformed to the Gold contents and accepted as legal tender. There was no free gold market. The local currency was convertible into foreign exchange based on gold. Bank notes were freely and unconditionally exchangeable for Gold and Gold was used in the settlement of international payments.

Gold standard was also not free from problems like inflexibility, little opportunity to avoid pressure for recession, overprinting of currency in excess of revenue to meet budget expenditure, inability of the system to absorb the disequilibrium situations. First World War disrupted the process and brought an end to Gold Standard. Major economies stopped trading with counterparts in Gold. Attempts were made for bringing back the system of payment but hyperinflation, devaluation, unemployment led to depression thereby discarding the Gold Standard.

Until the World War II, the depression continued in the world major economies spilling over the effects to other countries. However at the end of War, the European and their counterparts moved to restore an order in the world trade and attempted to recover the world economies by putting in place a free, stable and multilateral International Monetary system. A Monetary and Financial Conference was held at the UN in July, 1944, at **Bretton Woods**, New Hampshire, USA. Two organizations were established i.e. International Monetary Fund (IMF) and International Bank for Reconstruction and Development (World Bank). An agreement was reached, requiring all countries to fix the value of their currencies to Gold via US Dollars. Countries were required to exchange their currencies for dollars and dollar was to be convertible to gold at the request of the Central Banks as agent of their respective governments at the rate of US$ 35 per ounce. IMF was assigned the supervision of this system. Member countries were required to subscribe quantities of gold and local currencies according to their agreed quotas. This system of **Bretton Woods,** worked for more than 25 years until August 1971, when markets remained closed for many days.

USA suspended the fixed convertibility of US dollars and resultantly many currencies were allowed to float freely. This act led to instability. Realizing the danger, the "Group of Ten" (G-10) countries held a meeting and reached at an agreement "Smithsonian Agreement" in December 1971. The agreement raised the price of gold from $35 to $38 per ounce. Due to devaluation of currencies by some of the member countries the convertible rate was again raised to $42.22 per ounce but this system also could not sustained and only after a year the currencies were let to free float without any formal agreement.

The floating exchange rate system that evolved after 1973 in contravention of the IMF agreement, had abandoned the presence of official rates. Currencies were allowed to float freely against each other in a disorderly manner. IMF tried to bring order to the exchange rate by bringing the major currency holder to a table. But the break of Arab- Israeli war disbanded the efforts. The disruption brought in by the war led to the oil embargo which in turn led to the rise of oil prices which in turn caused international balance of payment issues. Intellectual and experts were divided on the issue of fixed rate and floating rate. Those in favor of the floating Exchange rate system advocated that floating add dimension to the economic flexibility, retain robust currency and favorable international balance of payment, rendering control over money supply, small amount of foreign reserve at Central Bank and little chance for speculations. On the other hand those in favor of the fixed exchange rate propounded that control of inflation is more important than independence of reserve and balance of payment. They contended that it was a fake idea that foreign reserve would be required minimum as practice and history revealed Central Bank's intervention and proved it otherwise. In practice, over the time it has been seen that fixed exchange rate and free floating cannot be exercised independently rather a marriage of both- "adjustable peg" would provide for periodic devaluation/ revaluation and "managed float" through Central Bank and central bank's intervention would be more workable and favorable.

Free float of currency happens when the currency rate are determined by the market forces of demand for the currency and supply of the currency in the foreign exchange market. Government does not intervene directly or indirectly in support of the currency and there is no need for large foreign currency reserves.

Managed float of currency happens when the currency rate is not determined by the market forces of demand for the currency and supply of the currency in the foreign exchange market. Government intervenes through Central Bank directly or indirectly in support of the currency. Central Bank intervenes at the time of undue fluctuation in the exchange rate or at the time to encourage exchange rate conducive to the balance of payment equilibrium. This is achieved by selling or purchasing the foreign currency against local currency or other foreign currency to bring the rate of exchange of the relevant currency against local currency to desired level of exchange.

FOREIGN EXCHANGE MARKETS

Sellers and Buyers (market participants) use Foreign Exchange Market (FX market) when they need to sell or purchase (convert) currencies. Like any market, the "Foreign Exchange Market" exists to allow buyer and seller of the goods (currency) in this case, to execute transaction and exchange their assets. Foreign Exchange Market typically refers to commercial Banks in large financial centers. The market participants use the FX Market when they need to convert one currency into another. Foreign Exchange Market differ from other familiar market in that the buyer and seller do not face each other in a particular place (Market Place) rather dealers in Foreign Exchange trading rooms conduct transactions by telephone and other sophisticated communication systems placed in the dealing rooms. In the Foreign Exchange market, the market place is the dealing room of commercial banks and brokers, linked by electronic communication systems to each other and to their customers.

A foreign exchange transaction is a contract to buy or sell a quantity of one currency in exchange for another at an agreed rate of exchange, for delivery on a specified date or period. The relative amount of each currency is determined by the Foreign Exchange rate between the two currencies. Foreign Exchange international market is the largest of its kind in the world with a reported daily volume of US$ 6.6 trillion each day. The main participants in the Foreign Exchange market are the major international banks. They deal in the market on behalf of their customers and speculatively for themselves. Other participants include brokers, investment institutions, corporate and central banks. Most Foreign Exchange transactions are inter-bank. Foreign Exchange transactions with non-bank customers and institutions account for one third of the daily turnover in the market.

FOREIGN EXCHANGE TRADING CENTRES

According to a report by the Bank for International Settlement (BIS), which monitors the activity of the world Money Market & Foreign Exchange Market based on surveys by central banks, over six and half trillion is traded on average every single day. Foreign Exchange is traded over-the-counter (OTC), operating worldwide 24 hours a day. A number of foreign exchange instruments, called derivatives (financial instrument; value of which is based on an underlying security) are traded on exchanges. The most active centers of Foreign Exchange are Singapore, Tokyo, Frankfurt, London, New York, Bahrain and Hong Kong. There are also other centers in other countries, e.g. Canada, Switzerland etc.

London is the world's largest FX centre whereas New York and Singapore are regarded 2nd and 3rd with respect to FX business volume. The trading times of the major FX markets almost span over 24 hours. The trading moves with clock (time) from one trading centre to the other with respect to time zone. FX business is executed in each centre in its normal working hours. It starts for example, in Singapore Hong Kong and Tokyo (Asia), almost in the same time zone and considered as the key centers in the Far East region. As the day moves on Bahrain (Middle East) wakes up and further in the early afternoon Frankfurt and London (Europe) starts working. At the end of the working day in London, market moves on to New York. Before close of business in New York it starts working in Sydney (Australia) and turns back to Singapore (Asia). So one day ends and another begins. All major Banks have branch network in all the Financial Centers and each centre is individually responsible for squaring its position or otherwise. It works 24 hours and moves through all continents. The major banks mostly deal in three time zones and execute customers order round the clock. The gap between the close of New York and the opening of Tokyo is usually covered by extended hours by the bank's dealing rooms. The transaction between the participants is based on trust, confidence and on an unwritten ethical agreement of commitment between the dealers. All the deals are recorded through the system for reference and audit trail is available for inspection.

FOREIGN EXCHANGE MARKET- PARTICIPANTS

By its practice and operations both Foreign Exchange and Money Market share characteristics like both the markets have no exclusive physical place of market and the participants of the market i.e. buyer and seller of foreign exchange do not need to come into physical contact. Deals and transactions are executed through common participant i.e. dealers of the dealing rooms through latest electronic communication systems and applications. Participants are largely Commercial Banks, Central Bank, Brokers and Corporations. The only difference is that in Foreign Exchange market only currencies are exchanged or traded whereas in Money Market foreign Exchange is lent or borrowed for interest earning (price of money). The major Participants are;

COMMERCIAL BANKS

Commercial Banks are considered among the primary market maker of a foreign exchange transaction. Banks provide, by default, a number of financial services to a large number of its clients. Therefore, Banks play a pivotal role in the foreign exchange market. Banks, when asked; quote a price on a two way basis (discussed later) i.e. Bid and Offer and are ready to either buy or sell in reasonable volume. Market has some customs, symbols and business ethics, without compromising on honesty, trust and confidentiality. For example a Box Bank is asked by Shelf Bank to quote a price. Depending on the position of Box Bank, it will quote a two way price i.e. Bid price (buying) and Offer price/ rate (selling) the currency being asked. The price shall always be competitive however; Shelf Bank would not indicate whether he is interested in buying or selling. If the price is good for Shelf Bank a deal may be struck otherwise, it is passed on by Shelf Bank. Foreign Exchange market works on the basis of reciprocity. Quote a good price and you will get a good price in return. The dealers support each other in squaring their daily positions. This fair trade and risk management gives them a high hope to make money from the trade.

CENTRAL BANKS

Every Country has a Central Bank. Central Bank is the regulatory body of a country for the control of monetary system. It works as an agent to the Government. Central bank supervises the banking and money transmission system. It controls the money supply and domestic interest rates and maintains stability of the exchange rate of the local currency. Central bank promotes the achievement of Govt. goals of economic growth, balance of trade, employment, price stability, inflation and foreign exchange reserves. These objectives are attained through monetary policy of the central bank. There are a number of methods used by central bank to implement its monetary policy. This subject is beyond the scope of this book; however a brief account may not be out of place to mention.

Open market operation (purchase and sale of Govt. securities with the aim to contract or expand the credit); hence control money supply.

Bank rate policy; Central bank controls money supply i.e. M1, M2, M3.

Statutory deposit ratio; Banks and financial institution are obliged to deposit a % age of their deposits with Central Bank. Central Bank can raise the % age rate or lower it to control money supply. Scheduled Banks can invest their reserves in Govt. securities subject to conditions.

Cash reserve requirements; Banks and financial institutions are obliged to deposit a prescribed % age of their time and demand liabilities with Central Bank. Bank can raise the % age or lower it to control money supply/credit.

Credit control; Central bank determines the margin on credits extended by commercial banks.

Sale/purchase of foreign exchange against local currency and import and export of foreign currency/banknotes; hence meet the need.

ADVISORY SERVICES

Some expert in the secondary market (market taker) follow the trends and sentiment in the foreign exchange market and issue their opinion on the trend of exchange rate movement in spot as well as forward investment in currencies. The expert may give solicited opinion and may publish their opinion on blogs and other print media and electronic media.

BROKERAGE HOUSES

Primary market makers are available with ways to quote their price to the market with and without identification. If a Commercial bank quotes its price to another counterpart, they know each other and ticket is generated mentioning both the parties. On the other hand a Commercial bank can ask or may quote a price to a broker without disclosing his identity to the market. Broker on comparing the rate so quoted by various dealers may float/ quote the most competitively good rate to the market. This would turn to be the primary rate for the day business. Brokers generally do not play as primary price makers rather they bring the two parties to a deal and just go out. If the deal is otherwise legal and permissible the two parties generate their deal ticket on each other and settle the transaction on the terms already agreed upon via broker. Broker provides service to vast majority of participants for commission and do not make the sale/purchase on their own account. Big brokerage houses provide such services round the clock all over the world as their business.

Chapter Two

FOREIGN EXCHANGE BASICS

SPOT EXCHANGE RATES

Exchange rates are simply the rates at which two different currencies are exchanged. Rate of exchange is the extent to which so many unit(s) of a currency of one country is exchanged for one unit of a currency of other country. In simple words Foreign Exchange rate can be defined as "the price of one currency in terms of another currency". For simplification and easy understanding, the major currencies of the world like; US dollar (USD), British Pound (GBP), Euro (EUR), Japanese Yen (JPY), Swiss franc (CHF), Australian dollar (AUD), Singaporean dollar (SGD) and Canadian dollar (CAD) shall be used in illustrations and examples.

Hence the rate of exchange between USD and GBP is expressed as USD / GBP = 0.8868. This shows that one USD is equivalent to or exchangeable for GBP 0.8868. Inversely 1GBP = 1/0.8868= USD 1.1277. If we need to purchase USD 100, we simply multiply USD 100 with GBP 0.8868 to reach at the total GBP value of USD 100 as; USD100 X 0.8868 = 88.68 GBP. Depending on the circumstances, one can express either currency as the price for the other and as such exchange rates can be quoted in "either direction".

The first currency i.e. on the left hand side is termed as <u>Base or Reference or First</u> currency and the one on the right hand side is termed as <u>Counter or Variable or Second</u> currency. The terms "Base currency & Counter currency" shall be used for reference hereinafter in the book.

Moreover, rates between GBP and USD can be expressed in the following two ways;

> ➢ The amount of GBP required to exchange for one USD as; 1USD = GBP 0.8868.
> It is expressed as USD/GBP 0.8868

> ➢ The amount of USD required to exchange for one unit of GBP as; GBP 1 = US$ 1.1277
> It is expressed as GBP/USD 1.1277

Similarly the exchange rate between USD and EUR can be expressed as;

> ➢ The amount of USD required to purchase one EUR as 1EUR = USD 0.9875

> ➢ The amount of EUR to be exchanged for one USD as 1USD = EUR 1.0127.

When there is only one rate given, it is called middle rate. Both sale and purchase is made by Bank and Broker at this single rate e.g. USD/GBP = 0.8868.

Certain assumptions are made for understanding foreign exchange while dealing with FX rates.

❖ In any exchange rate there are always two currencies involved at least. It means that there is a 'pair' of currencies to say, e.g. USD/GBP, EUR/GBP, JPY/ USD, and so on.

❖ In the pair of two currencies one is termed as "Base currency" of the pair (left) and other is called "Counter currency" of the pair (right). It is important to identify the position/expression of the currencies in the pair, as which one is "Base" currency and which one is "Counter" currency in the pair. Price makers and price takers base their deals on Base currency. When rate is quoted in the form USD/GBP 0.8868 (single rate), it is construed that; Table 2.1

Base Currency	Counter Currency	Mid Rate
USD	GBP	0.8868

For example in a pair that is expressed as US$/ GBP, here USD is the "Base" of the pair and GBP is the "Counter" currency of the pair. It is also useful to;

- Identify which currency is expressed in which one.
- Identify which currency is traded/sold or purchased.
- Identify the rates of sale and purchase being quoted.

❖ Exchange rates are always quoted in terms of Base currency as USD/GBP = 0.8868. It means that GBP as counter currency is expressed in USD. i.e. GBP 0.8868 is equal to of 1USD, the Base currency. Exchange rates are always quoted in terms of so many units of Counter currency per one unit of Base currency.

❖ Exchange rates are expressed up to four decimal places as shown in above example except for JPY and ITL. However, it is subject to the figures on the left side of decimal. In other word the strength of the unit of currency or monetary value of counter currency. If value at the left hand side of decimal is large, the decimal may be NIL or less than four. If value at the left hand side of decimal is small or zero, the decimal on left hand side may be four or more e.g.
Table 2.2

Base Currency	Counter Currency	Mid Rate
USD	JPY	148.9700
USD	EUR	0.9875

❖ Figure on the right hand side of the decimal i.e. 0.9875, in the above last pair USD/EUR, the first two digit shows the hundredth of the unit of EUR whereas the last two digits are called the basis points (pips) showing hundredth of the hundred. Exchange rate may be expressed in different forms as;

Table 2.3

Base Currency	Counter Currency	Middle rate or Mid Rate	Basis Points (pips)
USD	EUR	0.9875 or 0.98-6/8	6/8=.0075

DUALITY OF RATES- (Bid & Offer)

❖ As indicated above, practically foreign exchange rates are quoted in a set. One is called Bid rate or "Buying" rate and other Offer rate or "Selling" rate, e.g. USD/GBP 0.8868 - 0.8878. The first rate of the two is the Buying rate for Base currency- 1USD from the bank point of view, whereas it is the rate at which the client can sell to the bank (customer's perspective). The other rate of the two is the "Selling" rate of Base currency from the bank point of view and the rate at which client can buy (customer's perspective). For instance;

Table 2.4

Base Currency	Counter Currency	Bid/buying Rate	Offer/selling rate
USD	GBP	0.8868	0.8878

Here a point to be noted that the Bank (market maker) or an exchange dealer (market taker) transacts in foreign exchange for making money. This earning is twofold.

o Bank charges commission or tariff or fee for the transaction as services provided. (Vary from Bank to

Bank as per tariff). Exchange dealer commission is built in the rate quoted.

- o Bank sells at a higher rate and purchase at a lower rate. Thus keeping the difference (spread) as earning e.g. USD/GBP 0.8868 (Buying) – 0.8878 (Selling).

In this case Bank offers to sell one USD for GBP 0.8878 and purchase one USD for GBP0.8868. It indicates that there is difference of GBP 0.0010 in selling and purchase price. Bank charge more GBP for one US$ and give less GBP for one USD. This difference of 0.0010 is the spread for the bank. If a company/trader wishes to purchase 100 USD from the bank, he has to pay GBP 88.78 (100 X 0.8878). On the other hand a company/trader comes to sell US$ 100; he receives GBP 88.68 (100 X 0.8868). The difference of 0.10 (0.8878-0.8868) is the spread in the transaction for the bank. In heavy transactions this spread amounts to a reasonable figure. Like; USD/GBP 0.8868-0.8878.

Table 2.5

Base Currency	Counter Currency	Bid/buying Rate	Offer/selling rate	Spread
USD	GBP	0.8868	0.8878	0.0010

EXCHANGE RATE QUOTATION CONVENTIONS

As discussed above Foreign Exchange rate, between two currencies can be expressed in two ways as;

"The number of unit of USD required for one unit of GBP as GBP/USD = USD 1.1277"

"The number of unit of GBP required for one USD as USD/GBP = GBP 0.8868".

Trading of currencies in the foreign exchange markets, buying and selling of currency in a pair of currencies is expressed in two ways, i.e. Direct Quotation and Indirect Quotation. The difference depends upon identifying one currency as a domestic and other as a foreign currency.

DIRECT / EUROPEAN QUOTATION

Direct quotation is the variable number of units of <u>local currency</u> exchangeable for one (single) unit of <u>foreign currency</u>. For example from the perspective of a US participant, the local currency is USD and any other currency, such as GBP, EUR, JPY, etc. is foreign currency. From a perspective of a Canadian participant CAD is local currency and for a British participant, a GBP is a domestic whereas all others are foreign currencies. Market maker deals in base currency. Therefore, when the Base currency in the pair is a foreign currency, it is called Direct/European or Pence Rate Quotation, for example GBP/USD 1.1277 (Buying) – 1.1287 (Selling) for the sale purchase of GBP in US market. This is expressed as;

a) Direct Quotation in US Market GBP/ USD = 1.1277
b) Direct Quotation in UK Market USD/GBP = 0.8868

Suppose a customer possess 500 GBP currency/banknotes and want to sell it to the Bank in USA or wants to purchase USD against that bill. Conversely we put it in other way around that Bank want to purchase the banknotes or want to sell USD against the banknotes. What rate will be used to complete this transaction?

Base currency is a foreign currency GBP. Remember that bank deal in Base currency. The benefit of both the Bank and the Customer is conflicting as both desires the best in one's favor. But the Bank is at an advantageous position as it offers the rates (Price Maker). So it is in favor of the bank to give less USD for each GBP. Hence the rate for this transaction is the lowest one among the two being offered i.e. 1.1277. Customer receives USD 563.85 (GBP 500 x 1.1277).

Again suppose that the customer needs GBP 500. Here the Bank in USA will sell the GBP. It is in the interest of the Bank to get more USD for each GBP he sells to the customer. The rate to be applied in this situation is USD 1.1287. Customer pays USD 564.35 (GBP 500x1.1287). Hence the thumb rules to apply in case of direct quotation is BL-SH; **"BUY LOW- SELL HIGH"**

INDIRECT /AMERICAN TERMS QUOTATION

This type of quotation refers to the number of units of a foreign currency that can be exchanged for one (single) unit of a local currency, for example USD/GBP = GBP 0.8868 as quoted in US market. Looking at this from a British trader perspective in UK market, the number of units of a foreign currency, that can be exchanged for one unit of local currency i.e. GBP as in (a) above. UK uses this type of quotation in the Foreign Exchange market and use 365 days in a year for calculations. It means that when the Base currency of the pair is a local currency in the local market, it is an indirect/American or Currency Rate Quotation e.g. USD / GBP = 0.8868 - 0.8878 in US market and GBP/USD = USD 1.1277 -1.1287 in UK market.

a) Indirect quotation in US Market GBP/USD=0.8868-78
b) Indirect quotation in UK Market USD/GBP=1.1277-87

Suppose a customer of a Bank in US market possess 500 GBP banknotes and want to sell it to the bank or wants to purchase USD against those banknotes (for cash/ banknotes and account deposit or transfer transaction, rates are always different). Conversely we put it in other way around that Bank want to purchase banknotes or want to sell USD against the banknotes. What rate will be used to complete this transaction?

Base currency is a local currency USD. Remember that bank deal in Base currency. The benefit of both the Bank and Customer is conflicting again as both desires the best in one's favor. But the Bank is at an advantageous position as the Bank offers the rates (Price Maker). So it is in the favor of the Bank to receive more GBP for each unit of USD. Hence the rate for this transaction is the highest one among the two being offered (buying) i.e. 0.8878. Customer receives USD 563.19 (GBP 500 / 0.8878).

Suppose again that the customer needs GBP500. Here the Bank will purchase the US$. It is in the interest of the Bank to give less GBP for each unit of USD he purchases from the customer or take more dollars for each unit of GBP.

The rate to be applied in this situation is 0.8868. Customer pays USD 563.82 (GBP 500/0.8868). Hence the thumb rule here to apply is BH-SL; **"BUY HIGH-SELL LOW"**

REVERSING THE RATE

By reversing we mean that if a middle rate is given, which is expressed in term of Base Currency. How the rate in terms of Counter currency can be determined.

Given: USD/ JPY= 148.9750
Required:1 JPY=USD?

Calculation: 1 USD = JPY 148.9750
1 JPY =1/148.9750 (dividing)
1 JPY = US$ 0.00671

In case of dual rate, then how the rate in term of Counter currency can be calculated.

Given: USD/ JPY=148.9750 - 150.9750
Required: 1 JPY = USD?

Calculation: 1 USD =JPY 148.9750 - 150.9750

Transposing the figure of buying and selling before division:

1 JPY= 1/150.9750- 1/148.9750 (dividing after transposing)
1 JPY=USD 0.006624 - 0.006713

Given a direct quote GBP/USD = 1.1277 – 1.1287 in US market quotation, we can obtain an indirect quote by simply reversing the pair of currencies position as Base and Counter currency. For example direct quote by converting the quote, change the position of currency as;

GBP/USD =1.1277 – 1.1287
(Transpose the Buying & Selling)
=1.1287 – 1.1277

Suppose that under currency quote GBP/USD = 1.1277 – 1.1287 from a US market participant, a customer wants to sell GBP 500. What the bank does? To select the most favorable rate, keeping the spread of 0.0010, the rate at which bank is prepared to purchase is 1.1277, why, because bank will try to give less USD for same amount of GBP 500. So price in USD is 500 x 1.1277 = 563.85 USD

Oppositely the same customer changes his mind and ask for purchase of GBP 500, the rate of selling (Buying for customer) US$ by the bank will be 1.1287, which mean bank will try to take more USD for the same amount of GBP 500. So 500 X 1.1287 = 564.35USD. The difference of USD 0.50 (564.35-563.85) is the spread for the bank in the transaction.

CROSS RATES

US Dollar is the flagship currency in world even today despite the fact that China has outcast in terms of GNP and world trade. US Dollar is still the major trading currency in the world trade and in the foreseeable future the US currency shall remain as major currency in the global currency market. USD carries the confidence of world traders, accepted as a store of value and medium of exchange. USD is the main Foreign Exchange Reserve currency of almost all the Central Banks. GBP is quoted as reference currency in UK market as USD in US and rest of the world trade.

However, in the absence of any govt. restrictions, risk less arbitrage will assure that the exchange rate between two countries/currencies will be the same in both countries. The exchange rates between two currencies neither of which is USD or GBP is referred to as Cross rate. At times, clients and other Banks may often come across for business against currencies other than USD or GBP. Therefore it may be necessary to find out exchange rate between two currencies other than the USD or GBP. Although the rates between two specific currencies may not be quoted by the market, yet individually they may be quoted with reference to a third common currency. This common currency may be USD or GBP. The exchange rate can be inferred from their exchange rate with the USD or GBP. Such rate computed in this way, are referred to as theoretical cross rates. These can be computed through following methods;

OPPOSITE RULE METHOD

Step1. Identify the <u>common currency</u> in the two given/available pairs of rates.
Step2. Identify the position of the <u>common currency</u> as to whether it is Base or Counter currency of the pair. The common currency must be Base or Counter currency in both pairs.

Step3. In case where common currency is Base currency in one pair and Counter currency in other, simply <u>transpose</u> one of the pairs to bring it at common place by reversing the rate.

Step4. Look at the given two pairs of rate. If the common currency is Base currency in the given pairs, applying the opposite rule, it is the exchange rate of currency involving the Counter currency of <u>required cross rate</u> which is the numerator and goes on top of formula. On the other hand if the common currency is Counter currency in the given pairs, applying the opposite rule, it is the exchange rate of currency involving the Base currency of <u>required cross rate</u> which is the numerator and goes on top of formula.

Illustration: (steps expanded for simplification & clarity)

Given;
USD / GBP = 0.8868
EUR/ GBP = 0.8980
Required: USD/EUR - Cross rate

Step1. Find the <u>common currency</u> in the two given/available pairs of rates e.g. USD/GBP and EUR/ GBP, which is GBP, available in both pairs.

Step2. Find the position of the <u>common currency</u> as to whether it is Base or Counter currency of the pair. It is Counter currency in both the pairs.

Step3. In this case no need.

Step4. Using the opposite rule, identify the Base currency of <u>required cross rate</u> (USD/EUR) i.e. USD.

Step5. Look at the given two pairs of rate. Which rate contains USD? It is USD/GBP rate among the two rates given.

Step6. It is the numerator of the opposite rule method and goes on top of formula.

Therefore, putting the value; 0.8868/ 0.8980 = 0.9875
Hence the Cross rate USD/EUR is USD 1 = EUR 0.9875

Illustration: (step expanded for simplification & clarity)

Given
EUR / GBP = 0.9107
USD / EUR = 1.0127
Required: USD/GBP: Cross rate

Solution:

Step1. Find the <u>common currency</u> in the two given/available pairs of rates. It is EUR.
Step2. Find the position of the <u>common currency</u> as to whether it is Base or Counter currency of the pair. EUR is Base currency in EUR / GBP and Counter currency in USD / EUR.
Step3. <u>Transpose</u> one of the pairs. GBP/ EUR = 1/.9107 = 1.0981. Now common currency is the <u>Counter currency</u> in both pairs as;

GBP/ EUR=1.0981 and USD/ EUR=0.9875

Step4. Identify the <u>Base</u> (Opposite of common) currency of <u>required cross rate</u> using the opposite rule. It is USD.
Step5. Identify in the two pairs of rate (transposed). Which rate of the pair's contain- Base currency of <u>required cross rate</u>. It is USD/EUR.
Step6. USD/EUR rate is the numerator of the opposite rule method and goes on top of formula.

GBP/ EUR = 1.0981 and USD/ EUR = 0.9875

Hence the Cross rate USD/GBP = 0.9875/1.0981 = 0.8993

CHAIN EQUATION METHOD

Illustration:

Suppose that following rate quoted in New York for spot transaction against USD.
Given is;

USD/JPY =148.9750 – 150.9750
USD/AUD =1.5841 – 1.5851
USD/CAD =1.3705 – 1.3715
USD/EUR =1.0127 – 1.0137
GBP/USD =1.1277 – 1.1287

Your Customer has approached you with EUR. He desires to purchase CAD. The above Exchange rates do not contain exchange rate between these desired currencies. It is required to find the exchange rate between Canadian Dollar and Euro using the above given currency rates. Therefore;

CAD ? = 1 EUR
Where
EUR 1.0137=1 USD
USD 1= 1.3705 CAD

By applying the Chain Rule method;

CAD? = $\frac{1 \text{ EUR} \times 1 \text{ USD} \times 1.3705 \text{ CAD}}{\text{EURO } 1.0137 \times \text{US\$ } 1}$
=1 X 1 X 1.3705/ 1X1.0137
=1.3705/1.0137
=1.3520 CAD
Hence 1 EUR=1.3520 CAD

Alternatively, we have two equations as;

CAD ? = 1 EUR
Where
EUR1.0137= 1 USD-------- (1)
USD 1= 1.3705 CAD------- (2)

Rearrange equation no 1 and 2 by putting value of USD;

EUR 1.0137=1.3705 CAD

Since we need to calculate 1EUR equivalent to CAD? Therefore divide both side of equation by value of EUR 1.0137, to reduce it to 1 EUR

EUR 1.0137/1.0137=1.3705/1.0137 CAD

Hence; 1EUR=1.3520 CAD

Inversely, if asked to calculate 1CAD equivalent to EUR? Then divide both side of equation by 1.3705

EUR 1.0137= 1.3705 CAD
EUR 1.0137/1.3705= 1.3705/1.3705 CAD
0.73966 EUR = 1 CAD
Hence; 0.73966 EUR = 1 CAD

In this case we have two transactions;

Bank will purchase EUR against US dollars and give USD to customer so that he can Purchase CAD or in other words;

Bank will sell CAD against US Dollars

The whole transaction should be perceived with Bank's perspective. Bank is selling USD to the customer. Bank would apply the higher rate for USD against EUR i.e. 1.0137 (Sell High) taking more EUR from the customer against each USD. Then the Bank would purchase US dollar from customer against CAD giving less CAD against each dollar using the rate 1.3705 (Buy Low).

It is rare that cross rate, so calculated from actual dealer exchange rate quotes, will differ from the actual cross rates quoted by dealers. But if the difference is large with transaction cost of buying and selling the currencies, a risk less arbitrate (purchasing currency in one market and selling in other) is resorted to. This arbitrage is called "Triangular arbitrage", as it involves three currencies. Through such arbitrage the actual and theoretical cross rate are kept similar.

Bank may add or subtract margin as its profit. Such a situation depends on the quotation convention of rates by the bank i.e. Direct or Indirect quotation. Transaction cost or a profit margin for the bank. For direct quotation the rule apply is "Buy low Sell High" (BL-SH) therefore when buying the foreign currency, the earning margin or transaction cost to be recovered, should be deducted thereby further lowering the purchase price. On the other hand when selling the foreign currency, it should be added to the rate thereby increasing the selling rate. The scenario where rates are quoted under Indirect Convention, the Maxim applied here is "**Buy High Sell Low**" (BH-SL). Bank would buy at higher rate so make it more higher and vice versa.

FORWARD RATES

Since Foreign Exchange has evolved over time mainly to serve the purpose of international finance and trade. International payment has led to exchange of currencies owing to variation in global currencies. Foreign exchange can be bought and sold not only in ready/spot market i.e. for immediate delivery but also on a forward basis i.e. for delivery on a stipulated future date. Thus Forward rate has been developed to cater the commercial requirements of the international traders. The traders become able to fix the cost of their imports and revenue of their exports in terms of domestic currency in advance of the due date/time of the actual payment or receipt when converted thereby securing themselves from any adverse fluctuation in exchange rates.

Forward exchange contract is therefore one whereby the rate of future receipt or payment is fixed spot/today for purchase or sale of one currency against another for actual delivery at some agreed future date or period. Such date of settlement can be anywhere from the deal date to several years forward. Forward foreign exchange transaction is a non negotiable and traded over the counter. No funds are exchanged on the deal date. Therefore the forward market is the market where parties negotiate to buy and sell foreign currencies for delivery at a specified future date/ period. The period may be long or short but generally and most practically, it is dealt for a short period of one month to one year's time. Even if a customer asks for a different period, bank will quote for any maturity date called "broken period".

Theoretically, the forward price for a currency can be identical to spot rate, however, these are rarely the same as the spot rates. The exchange rate deal settling on the day other than the usual spot date i.e. a day or two hence, has two basic components. One is the spot rate itself. Deal done on this date is referred to as Cash transaction. Other component is the interest rate differential for a different date of settlement. This deal is referred to as Forward transaction/contract. Therefore, Forward prices are derived from spot prices but these may be higher than spot by adding interest differential as a premium or less than spot by deducting interest differential as discount. It reflects difference in interest rates on deposits prevailing in the counties of currencies involved. Forward rates are not based on prediction regarding the future spot rate but the interest rates in the countries of the currencies involved in the transaction.

Depending on the time zone of the counter parties, value date may be the day of deal or day of deal +1 or it can be the day of deal+2. This is spot deal among the professional traders. Further the spot next value date is the day of deal +2 or the day of deal +3. The deal beyond these dates/days is regarded as Forward deal by the professional foreign exchange dealers. Forward contracts of foreign exchange are used in a number of scenarios and serve different purposes. These deals can be used to hedge against exchange risk whether commercial in nature or financial. Forward exchange rates and its mechanics can be explained through example to understand.

> Suppose that an importer in UK has imported goods from an exporter in US. The payment of 500,000 USD is due after three months time (90 days). Further suppose that interest rates prevailing in both the markets are; suppose;

Table 2.6

Period	USD	GBP
3 months CD rate	3%	6%
Spot selling GBP/USD	1.1277	

There is 3% differential i.e. higher the interest rate in UK market as compared to US market. Customer asks his Box Bank for forward contract of delivery of USD against GBP after three months, the due date for payment to exporter. The Bank has two options i.e. wait until the date of delivery of dollars and do nothing. This is risky, because the exchange rates can fluctuate either way in favor of the bank or against the Bank. He may loose on the contract as compared to spot or may gain and vice versa for customer. Box Bank will have to secure itself by covering the deal in a way that;

Scenario No.1

Formula for calculation of forward points from interest differential;
Spot rate X Interest rate differential in decimal X term period
Basis/Total days in a year/ months in a year; USD 360 and for GBP 365 days of a year are taken in calculations).

Table 2.7

S.#	Particulars	Currency USD
1.	**Box Bank** purchased USD at spot rate against' GBP 443,380 (500000/1.1277 round figures).	500,000
2.	**Box Bank** invest USD @3% p.a for 3 Months (500000*.03*90/360), Interest earned for 3 months	3,750
3.	**Box Bank** has booked 3 months forward & sold the USD to a customer,	--
4.	**Box Bank** opportunity cost; GBP used for spot purchase of USD, If otherwise invested @6%, GBP 443,380*.06*90/360 would earned = GBP 6,651. Convert to USD 6,651*1.1277	(7,500)
5.	**Net**	496,250

Forward rate USD 496,250/443,380=1.1192.

33

Difference with spot rate =1.1277-1.1192= 0.00846.
This is what we call interest differential and used as Forward margin/points. Alternatively 1.1277*.03*90/360= 0.00846

Since Box Bank has actually lost on the transaction due interest differential, therefore Box Bank will offer fewer dollar against fixed GBP or fixed dollars against more GBP and vice versa. In this deal the forward rate will be less than the spot to make good the loss pocketed due to interest differential.

Scenario No.2;- Suppose that an importer in US has imported goods from an exporter in Switzerland. The payment of 500,000 CHF is due after three months time (90 days). Further suppose that interest rates prevailing in both the market are;

Table 2.8

Period	USD		CHF
3 months CD rate	3%		4%
Spot selling GBP/CHF		1.00471	

Customer asks his Shelf Bank for forward contract of delivery of CHF against USD after three months for payment to exporter. Shelf Bank will have to secure itself by covering the deal in a way that;

Table 2.9

S.#	Particulars	Currency CHF
1.	**Shelf Bank** purchased CHF at spot rate against' USD 497,656 (500000/1.00471 round figures).	500,000
2.	**Shelf Bank** invest CHF @4% p.a for 3 Months (500000*.04*90/360), Interest earned for 3 months	5,000
3.	**Shelf Bank** has booked 3 months forward & sold the CHF to a customer,	--
4.	**Shelf Bank's** opportunity cost; USD used for purchase of CHF, @3%,USD 497,656*.03*90/360,= USD 3732.42.Convert to CHF, 3,732.42 *1.00471	(3,750)
5.	**Net**	501,250

Forward rate USD 501,250/497,656= 1.00722. Check the difference 1.00722-1.00471 =0.00251. This is interest differential and is used as Forward margin/points. Alternatively 1.00471*.01*90/360= 0.00251

Since Shelf Bank has actually gained on the transaction due to interest differential, therefore Shelf Bank will offer more CHF against fixed USD or fixed CHF against less USD and vice versa. In this deal the forward rate will be more than the spot to transfer the gain to customer.

However, the basis of forward rate as discussed above is the earning power of the currency in different markets; there are other factors that play an important role in pricing the currency.

FORWARD RATE QUOTATION- TWO WAY

Foreign Exchange, as we know, is traded in the foreign exchange market as a commodity like in any other market. It is bought and sold at a price which is the rate of exchange of the commodity i.e. currency. Therefore, rate is always quoted in two ways for purchase of currency; "Bid rate" for buying and "Offer rate" for sale of currency. Likewise in forward contracts, trader needs two rates to be quoted for sale/purchase. It has to be recognized that the underlying market behind forward points (interest differential) is also traded on a bid - & - offer basis. However, in the foreign exchange market outright/full forward rates are not quoted, rather forward margins are quoted as an indicator of interest rate differential. Forward rates are calculated by adding or subtracting the points to/from the spot rates. The addition and/or subtraction indicate the "Premium" or "Discount", and indicated by the order of quotation of points. The term premium and discount can have different implication in different situation or rate quotation convention. Each point in forward quotation represent hundredth of hundred i.e. 1/100x100= 1/10000= 0.0001. These are quoted as under;

For example, spot GBP/USD is 1.1277- 1.1287 or expressed in a way as market practice i.e. 1.1277-10.

Table 2.10

Currency	Spot Rate	Quotation Style
GBP/USD	1.1277 – 1.1287 Or 1.1277 – 10	
Forward Margin (pips)		
One Month	25-30	Low to High
Three Months	75-95	Low to High

In this example the margins quoted, look very simple. It is quoted from low to high, means low for bid rate and high for offer rate but there is a question as to whether the margin is to be added to or subtracted from the spot. This is important to remember and worth noting. When margin quoted in this pattern/format i.e. from low to high, it is (margin) always meant to be **added** to spot rate to arrive at the outright forward rate as discount.

Table 2.11

Particulars	Bid Rate	Offer Rate	Rule	Difference
Spot Rate; GBP/USD	1.1277	1.1287	Add Margin	0.0010
Forward Margin: One Month	0.0025	0.0030		0.0005
Forward Rate: One Month	1.1302	1.1317		0.0015
Spot Rate; GBP/USD	1.1277	1.1287	Add Margin	0.0010
Forward Margin: Three Month	0.0075	0.0095		0.0020
Forward Rate: Three Month	1.1352	1.1382		0.0030

Two points to be noted in this example for further clarification. The marginal difference is greater in forward rates as compared to spot rate as shown in the last column. If by mistake, these margins are deducted from spot rate the difference will turn narrow and one can easily detect the mistake for correction e.g.

Table 2.12

Particulars	Bid Rate	Offer Rate	Rule	Difference
Spot Rate; GBP/USD	1.1277	1.1287	By mistake deducted Margin	0.0010
Forward Margin: One Month	0.0025	0.0030		0.0005
Forward Rate: One Month	1.1252	1.1257		0.0005
Forward Margin: Three Month	0.0075	0.0095	By mistake deducted Margin	0.0020
Forward Rate: Three Month	1.1202	1.1192		0.0010

One month forward bid rate is 1.1277 minus by mistake 0.0025= 1.1252 and one month forward offer rate is 1.1287 minus by mistake 0.0030=1.1257. The margin narrowed to 0.0005 only.

Three month forward bid rate is 1.1277 minus by mistake .0075= 1.1202 and three month forward offer rate is 1.1287 minus by mistake 0.0095=1.1192. The margin narrowed to 0.0010 only.

Forward rates are always higher than the spot rates. In this example, the GBP is at premium in the forward market as compared to USD (depreciated). Conversely USD is at discount in the forward market as compared to GBP. Therefore;

> GBP is at Premium in the forward market.
> USD is at discount in the forward market.

When the rate is quoted from low for bid and high for offer, then the base currency is at premium while the counter

currency is at discount. This is applicable to the pair in question. For a different pair the terms shall be different. To ascertain as to how much USD depreciated?
Table 2.13

Particulars	Bid Rate	Offer Rate	Rule	Difference
Spot Rate; GBP/USD	1.1277	1.1287	Add Margin	0.0010
Forward Margin: Three Month	0.0075	0.0095		0.0020
Forward Rate: Three Month	1.1352	1.1382		0.0030

Let us express the discount point in % age as = 75/(1.1277x 100x100) = 0.00665% rate of depreciation. Hence forward rate can be deduced as; = spot buying x (1+ % depreciation) = 1.1277x 1.00665.
Hence three months Forward rate = 1.1352.

Let see the other side of the coin: Suppose the quotation is; Table 2.14

Currency	Spot Rate	Quotation Style
GBP/USD	1.1277 – 1.1287 Or 1.1277 – 10	
Forward Margin (pips)		
One Month	30-25	High to Low
Three Months	95-75	High to Low

In this example the margin from high to low, means high for bid rate and low for offer rate but again there is a question as to whether the margin is to be added to, or subtracted from the spot. This is important to remember. When margin is quoted in this form/pattern of high to low, in such a situation, margin is always meant to be **subtracted** from spot rate as premium. Let suppose spot rate is 1.1277-1.1287.

Table 2.15

Particulars	Bid Rate	Offer Rate	Rule	Difference
Spot Rate; GBP/USD	1.1277	1.1287		0.0010
Forward Margin: One Month	0.0030	0.0025	Deduct Margin	0.0005
Forward Rate: One Month	1.1247	1.1262		0.0015
Forward Margin: Three Month	0.0095	0.0075	Deduct Margin	0.0020
Forward Rate: Three Month	1.1182	1.1212		0.0030

Two points to be noted in this example for further clarification.

The marginal difference is greater in forward rates as compared to spot rate as shown in the last column.

One month forward bid rate is 1.1277, if added by mistake 0.0030 would result = 1.1307 and one month forward offer rate 1.1287 is added by mistake 0.0025=1.1312. The margin narrowed to 0.0005 (1.1312-1.1307) only whereas actual spread was 0.0015.

Forward rates are always lower than the spot rates. Here the USD is expensive (appreciated) in the forward market against GBP. Conversely GBP is cheaper (depreciated) in the forward market against USD. Therefore;

- ➢ USD is at Premium in the forward market.
- ➢ GBP is at discount in the forward market.

When the rate is quoted as High for bid and Low for offer, then the base currency is at discount while the counter currency is at Premium. To ascertain as to how much USD appreciated?

Table 2.16

Particulars	Bid Rate	Offer Rate	Rule	Difference
Spot Rate; GBP/USD	1.1277	1.1287	Deduct Margin	0.0010
Forward Margin: Three Month	0.0095	0.0075		0.0020
Forward Rate: Three Month	1.1182	1.1212		0.0030

Difference in spread is 0.0030.
Let us express the premium point in % age as; = 95/ (1.1277x 100x100) = 0.00842% rate of appreciation.
Hence forward rate can be deduced as = spot buying x (1- % appreciation) = 1.1277(1-0.00842) =1.1277*0.9916= 1.1182. Three months forward rate = 1.1182.

Premium does not mean any extra value nor does it denote that the currency is cheap. It depends in which quotation the rate is quoted. If a currency is at premium in direct quotation, it will be at discount in indirect quotation. It should be noted that interest differential define the premium and discount. The currency of a country with lower interest rate will usually be quoted at premium in the forward market against the currency of a country with higher interest rate and a currency of a country with higher interest rate will be priced at a discount against the currency of a country with a lower interest rate.

FORWARD WITH FIXED AND OPTIONAL DATES

Fixed date forward is used extensively in foreign exchange market. As discussed in the earlier section when contract specifies delivery of contracted currency at a specified date in future it is called "Fixed Forward Contract". It has to be completed at the specified future date. A typical option dated forward contracts provide an opportunity to a corporate client to sell or buy a currency for delivery at any time at the option period. It is designed to serve their peculiar requirements. The option relates only to the date to complete the transaction. Delivery can be completed in total on one day or a number of partial deliveries can be made throughout the option period. But delivery must be completed on the last date of contract.

Suppose an importer enters into a three months forward purchase contract with his Bank;

•Importer asks for delivery of foreign currency with **full option**. It means that customer can take up the contracted currency amount on any business day within three month period. Or

•Importer may enter into a three month forward option contract with a two month option. It means to take up the foreign currency on any business day during the second and third/last month of the contract. Or

•Importer may enter into a three month forward option contract with a one month option. It means to take up the foreign currency on any business day during the third/last month of the contract. Similarly this can be exercised by exporter for sale of his export proceed.

FACTORS AFFECTING FORWARD POINTS

We know that spot rate is the basis for calculation of forward rates. If the spot rate for GBP/USD is 1.1277 and forward rate is 1.1192 as in the Scenario No.1, page 33, the difference of 0.00846 is referred to as forward points. A number of factors determine the size of points spread between spot and forward rate.

41

- Demand for and supply of the currency; if the buyers are greater in number, supply will be short and currency is hot, for demand is high and supply is constant or low. If on the other hand sellers are dominant in the market, supply is more and demand is little hence currency is cheap. Things available in abundance in the market are always cheap as per economics law of Demand and Supply.

- Market expectation regarding changes in interest rate and foreign exchange rates in the future.

- Difference in the rate of return (interest rates) on the currencies in respective countries of the currencies.

- Tenure of the contract straddling in the future, the farther is the contract date in future the larger is the actual amount of net interest due to interest rate differential.

DETERMINANTS OF FX RATES

Exchange rates are volatile to the extent that sometime the loss to some and profit to others due to such changes would be unmanageable. None of the participants are able to control such changes or can forecast through analysis of the past trends or experiences nor through the study of market forces alone. An investor trades in foreign exchange market with an aim to make profit, otherwise one can place his money in treasury bills (TBs) and earn say' 7 % for instance. Trading in exchange market must bring an earning more than the return on TBs or such other safe and secure investments. Taking risk entails profit but loss cannot be ignored, if there is no profit, no trading in FX may be a wise decision.

The prices of currencies are like prices of any other commodity. Commodities respond to market forces i.e. supply and demand of certain commodity. Therefore, if for instance there are only buyers in the market of a certain currency say "USD" keeping supply of dollar in the market as constant, price of USD shall definitely increase. USD shall appreciate in that market. Conversely, if there are only sellers in the market of USD, keeping the demand constant, at a point there shall no extra demand and the price of USD will decrease and resultantly depreciates USD in that market. There are many factors that contribute to forecast the movement in foreign exchange rate of a currency. Supply of and demand for a currency is also a function of many forces working round the clock in determining the rate of exchange of a currency in the world market.

PURCHASING POWER PARITY (INFLATION)

As mentioned in the intro of FX, if the same amount of currency in one country purchases the same amount of goods in all other countries, then there is no point in international trade and exchange rate variation. But the actual business and currencies do not behave in such a way.

Governments intervene to regulate the money supply thereby attaining the desired domestic price stability in the country. Such measures by the government also affect the foreign exchange rate of currency through the linkage in price and inflation in the country. This linkage is termed as Purchasing Power Parity (PPP).

Purchasing Power Parity is a measure of the relative purchasing power of different currencies. This principle was propounded by ***Gustav Cassell*** during 1920s. It states that exchange rates move to effectively bring about purchasing power parity between the currencies of different countries. The concept behind the theory is that if there is difference in purchasing power of currencies then it is profitable to export the goods from the country where these are cheap to a country where they are expensive.

For example Gucci wrist watch is CHF 1500 in Switzerland and USD 900 in USA. If the exchange rate is USD/CHF= 1.5. The watch in Switzerland will cost USD 1000 (1500/1.5). Therefore the US citizen is better off to purchase the watch in USA at a price of USD 900. If the rate between the two currencies changes to CHF 2.00 per USD, then the price in Switzerland will come to 750 USD. The buyer shall be better off to import from Switzerland (Ceteris Paribus). The watch is expansive in USA and one can purchase it in Switzerland. Therefore inflation duly affects the exchange rate of a currency in the long run. The rationale behind the theory begins with the law of one price. It states that price of a good in one currency, times the exchange rates, equal the price of same good in other currency. It is considering the connection between exchange rates and local currency price of an individual commodity in different countries. This connection between exchange rate and commodity price is known as the Law of one price.

Suppose that the price of a Car in UK is GBP10, 000. Further suppose that spot rate of GBP/ USD = 1.1277. The law of one price suggest that the US Dollar Price of the same good i.e. Car will be GBP 10,000 x 1.1277 = USD 11,277. The reason behind the law of one price is the arbitrage. The Car is available otherwise in US market at USD 10,500 which means that it could be bought in the US market at GBP 9,311 (10,500/1.1277). Car is cheap in US. It can be exported to UK where it can earn a profit of GBP 689(10,000– 9,311). This situation would not last for long. Because the demand for the Car would increase in the US for profitable export which would increase its price and on the other hand create an increase in supply to UK would decrease its price by eliminating the spread margin. The forces of market i.e.

demand and supply would continue to operate until the law of one price hold good. However, trade between the countries is not that easy. There are other trade barriers like, transportation cost, marketing cost, taxes and duties etc.

Suppose that PPP law operates for almost all the goods in both markets (Ceteris Paribus). Suppose further that inflation rate in US and UK market is 7% and 5%. Referring to our Car example, the price of the Car (keeping inflation rate constant for one year) in UK will be 10,000+ (10,000x 0.05) = GBP10, 500 and in US 11,277+ (11,277x 0.07) = 12,066 USD. The rate of exchange will be, 12,066/10,500 = 1.1492. This is law of one price, where inflation adjustment brings about change in exchange rates to maintain purchasing power parity between the trading currencies. This inflation differential in different countries defines the future spot rates. The currency of a country with lower inflation rate will usually be quoted at premium in the forward market against the currency of a country with higher inflation rate and a currency of a country with higher Inflation rate will be priced at a discount against the currency of a country with a lower inflation rate on the line effects as true with IRPT.

As the inflation rate is constant for a while and it is 5% in UK and 7% in US i.e. 7 – 5 = 2%, Inflation is lower by 2% in US as against in UK which indicates that next year USD will lose value and depreciate approximately by 2% against GBP i.e. the inflation differential as against GBP. It can be calculated as under; Rate of exchange is GBP/USD= 1.1277, where GBP is Base currency and USD is Counter currency.
US Inflation rate-UK Inflation rate/ divided by 1+ UK Inflation rate = % Change in US= = 0.07 – 0.05/1+ 0.05= 0.01905 X100= 1.905% =1.1277 (1 + 0.01905) =1.1492
Spot rate after one year.

BALANCE OF PAYMENTS

Terms of trade and amount of trade play an important role in the exchange rate of a currency. Government intervention through monetary and fiscal policies affect the balance of trade and therefore balance of trade is the most direct determinant of for the external value of the currency of the country. Balance of payment affect the supply and demand for currency through both the price and an income effect. Exports increases demand for currency and imports increase use of foreign currency. If imports into the country are greater than exports in terms of a currency e.g. USD, the Demand for a USD will increase thereby raising its value in relation to domestic currency and vice versa. USD will not only appreciate in spot but also in forward contract to cater to the importers demand for USD. An adverse Balance of payment results in fall in the exchange value of local currency and vice versa.

INTEREST RATES

The interest rate differential will entice the investor to maximize their return on investment in securities and convert local currency in the currency of the country where the interest rate is high. Purchasing the currency will increase its demand and resultantly the exchange rate will move up in favor of the currency of that country. Again the effect of demand and supply law will hold good and exchange rate will fluctuate. Rising interest rates will strengthen a currency by attracting more capital. However capital inflow will in turn affect the exchange rate in turn will affect exports.

The question of determination of Forward rates is basically answered by Interest Rate Parity Theory. IRP state that there is no bargain on the rate of interest on loan / deposit in one currency then another. You may benefit from the difference of interest rate for one currency but may lose in the exchange rate. Literally, exchange rates moves too effectively to bring about interest rate parity among different currencies. Suppose that spot rate GBP/USD =1.1277-1.1287 and 12 Months forward rate (forward margin 330/326) High to Low =1.0947-1.0961. Suppose that Treasury Bills in USA pay 4% and UK it Pays 7% and Investor wish to place GBP10,000/-in risk free deposit for one year. To decide whether to place in UK or in USA which one will be more profitable? IRPT say that it makes no difference the result will be the same and the high rate of return will be equalized by the exchange rate differential as;

GBP 10,000 deposit in UK TBs will yield after one year GBP Principal GBP 10,000+ (10,000x0.07) = GBP 10700/- Investment in US in TBs, investor need to purchase US$ at the spot rate and then place in US TBs. Covert GBP in USD=GBP10,000 x 1.1277=USD 11277. After one year it comes to USD 11277+ (11277x0.04) = USD 11728. Investor after one year converts the USD in GBP which gives at the spot rate after one year GBP 10700/ as after one year the rate of exchange is; GBP/USD 1.0947 - 1.0961. USD 11728 / 1.0961= GBP 10,699.75 (due to rounding of). Alternatively USD 11728/ 10700= 1.0961

This shows that investor is not better off after one year taking into account the exchange variation. Investor received what he would have received had kept the money on sterling deposit. This is how the forward exchange rates are defined to effectively bring about parity between interest rates in different currencies. The forward rate of the currency of the country with the lower rate of interest will appreciate against the currency of the country with the higher rate of interest by approximately the interest differential i.e. 7% - 4% = 3%. It can be calculated as under; Rate of exchange is GBP/USD= 1.1277, where GBP is Base currency and USD is Counter currency. Note that in the pair of GBP/USD the GBP is the Base currency and USD is the counter currency as; USD Interest rate – GBP Interest rate/ divided by 1+ GBP Interest rate = % Change in US GBP =0.04 – 0.07/1+ 0.07 = -0.02804 x100 = -2.804%

USD will change by -2.804 %. Here a question arises that whether USD is appreciated or depreciated against GBP. This increase is a discount or premium. Again to restate the forward rate of the currency of the country with the lower rate of interest will appreciate against the currency of the country with the higher rate of interest by approximately the interest differential. If the result is negative (-) it means it will appreciate against GBP. On the other hand if the result is positive it means it will depreciate against the GBP=1.1277+(1.1277x(-0.02804) =1.0961(USD appreciated against GBP.

POLITICAL AND PSYCHOLOGICAL

Political and psychological factors affect the exchange rate in that some of the currencies in world market are considered as a strong store of value, a currency of security/ refuge like USD, GBP, and CHF. No matter in which corner of the world, there is political disturbance, the locals of that country will secure their assets in USD or EURO, GBP, the currencies regarded and perceived secure. Market sentiment regarding changes in exchange rates of a currency some cause fluctuation in exchange rates due to the positive or negative sentiment of the market participants.

TECHNICAL

Sometime market participant act on the basis of their knowledge of fact and figure of the past trend in exchange rates movement. History repeats itself time and again. Technical analysis of trends takes into account the volume, futures market and prices. They assume that market participant will react the same way as they did in the past. Government regulation may sometime change the exchange rate for a short time for supporting local currency.

Chapter Three

FOREIGN EXCHANGE INSTRUMENTS

SPOT FX TRANSACTIONS

Foreign exchange can be an exchange of currencies/banknotes (Cash business- retailing) or sale /purchase of balances in deposit accounts (transfer).

FX RETAIL TRANSACTIONS

Citizens of a country are well familiar with the currency of their country. May it be a US citizen who knows the legal tender in US is a Dollar bill (blue back) or banknote or a UK and Swiss citizen who knows that Pound Sterling is a legal currency in UK and Swiss Franc is a legal tender in Switzerland. These citizens can shop in their respective countries with the respective banknotes or legal currency of their countries. But what if, a US citizen plans to go to Switzerland for vacation and a German citizen plans to travel to UK for studies and UK citizen plans to visit US with respect to business trip. Here the foreign exchange intervenes.

Those who plan to visit a foreign country shall arrange for the currency of the intended country to meet one's expenses in that country. There may be tens of reasons where a citizen needs to purchase or sell foreign currency in a country. The traveler shall visit a bank or an authorized money changer. Banks and other traders in currencies quote two rates for a currency as discussed earlier. One is for purchase and other for sale (Bid & Offer). The spread for bank in this case of banknote business is higher as compared to wholesale FX market for many reasons;

- The transaction is small.
- Cash currency does not earn any income.
- Mobility of cash entails cost of transportation, and cost of transit insurance.
- Chances of Counterfeit currency exchanged.
- Misappropriation, embezzlement, dacoit and street snatch etc.

Retail market is not that big rather it constitutes a small portion of spot market but cannot be ignored as it is an activity in foreign exchange market. Currency notes or other instruments denominated in foreign currency i.e. traveler's cheques; prepaid FX cards etc. are bought and sold by banks and authorized dealers. These balances are than exchanged with other banks or exported to the country of origin. Keeping large balances in different currencies cause loss to the entity. There are checks on cash balance from regulators and also the controlling offices of banks etc. In some countries these are surrendered to the central bank which arranges export of the same to the wholesale market to convert it into account as foreign reserves. The need of currency notes is the reverse of export i.e. imports by banks and/ or central bank from the wholesale market of such currencies needed by the citizens for different use at their end.

FX WHOLESALE TRANSACTIONS

Spot foreign exchange transactions are those transactions where F.C. is sold/ purchased for immediate delivery i.e. within two business days, excluding transaction date. Although spot markets exist for most of the world currencies, but many minor currencies does not trade spot/forward because of the insufficient demand? Spot rate of exchange is determined by the market forces i.e. demand for and supply of a currency.

Currency market is the largest in the world then the trade/commodity market. Trillion of USD changes hands/accounts and markets and thousands of transaction take place at each centre rather in each dealing room of every first class bank in the world.

DEALERS AND THE DEALING ROOMS

Dealers are specialist/experts of FX market. Dealing room size and number of dealers in the room depends on the size, volume and variety of FX business undertaken by the bank or brokerage house. A full-fledge dealing room contain specialized dealers in FX and Money market. There is a dealer for each activity of Spot desk (a separate dealer for each currency), Forward desk dealing in forward FX contracts and derivatives business in FX market. Similarly, there is a separate dealer dealing in money market and Client business desk (individual/corporate) in a dealing room of a bank or brokerage house. All the dealers report to the Chief Dealer as per Organ gram. A simple form in which one dealer is looking after the whole business of the FX transaction shall be considered henceforth for making the understanding simple.

FOREIGN EXCHANGE DEAL

At start of the business in the morning, depending upon the size, establishment and administrative set up of each individual bank, the financial dealer, based on the information of the world currencies and other related facts such as Political, Economic, Budget position, Balance of payment, monetary policies etc. workout exchange of sale and purchase of all major currencies. Telephonic, Tele printer, WhatsApp', internet contacts are made to other dealer and he is contacted by others regarding exchange rates for the day.

At the dealing room of "Box Bank" (BB), the dealer is provided with all the gadgets, Internet, computers, printers, scanner, dedicated screen like Telerate, Reuter 2000-1, 2000-2 and Tele-communication systems. It is notable that dealing room is a no go area in the premises of bank for unauthorized personnel. Controlled access to the room is restricted by security systems and only authorized personnel with access to computers is restricted and authorized.

The dealer needs to have FX rate, Bank deposit rates of various maturities and news and sentiment of the market. Dealer also maintains his dairy (manual/ electronic/ blotter) of daily list (value dated) of receivable from and payable to, of the day and balance with correspondent bank with foreign exchange exposure limit.

Dealing can be done in many ways available but the most practiced forms of dealing are;

- Over the Counter (OTC): Dealer to dealer conversation on phone.
- Electronic Trading: using the dedicated line of Reuter Screen, Telerate and brokerage service for reference.
- A voice broker: on the floor of the exchange through Hand Signals and outcry.

Monday, Sept 03, 20X2 for example, in the morning the dealer of Box Bank (BB) opens his diary i.e. Deal sheets, Deals Blotters, or Position of the day and go through the receivable and payable. He encircles a GBP receivable to be sold for USD. This amount is a daily collection of borrower M/s High Fly Airline (HFA). HFA has pledged as security and repayment to be appropriated at the end of each month for the loan in USD enjoyed by HFA. There are many collection points in different countries of the HFA in local currency of that country. BB as per contract collects the daily collections from the Collection accounts of HFA and converts the currencies into USD and pools it in account of

HFA with BB. BB at the end of month recovers the installment amount and allow HFA to use the over and above balance amount in the account. Dealer was supposed to sell GBP against USD. Following rate are available for the sale/ purchase of USD against GBP (cable rate) in the market. Spot is;
GBP/ USD = 1.1277/87

Dealer in BB calls dealer in **Shelf Bank (SB)** enquiring cable.

Dealer of BB, Hello Mr. I need cable in one dollar

Dealer of SB says 75/85'

Dealer in BB, Mr. I buy one dollar at "75".

Dealer of SB says, OK, I sell you one million dollar at 1.1275, value 5th September, thanks & regards.

After the above discussion some very important points need to be highlighted;

BB dealer asks for Cable rate; this term is used by the market for GBP/USD pair. Likewise USD/CHF as "Swissy", USD/JPY as "Gopher", USD/CAD as "Loonie" or Fund, EUR/GBP as "Chunnel" & "Guppy", USD/EUR as "Fiber", EUR/JPY as "Yuppy" etc.

While asking for rates, dealer at BB has kept silent as to whether he is a purchaser or seller. Otherwise the rate would have been slightly different.

SB dealer has quoted the rate in "pips". This is because the big figure (1.12) is known to both dealers. It is understood that big figure of big currencies do not changed overnight.

Both dealer know that first (left) pips (75) are for purchase i.e. Bid rate quoted by the SB dealer and large pips (85) is for sale i.e. Offer by the dealer. This means that SB dealer is ready to purchase base currency (GBP) at 1.1275 and sell base currency GBP at 1.1285. After receipt of quote,

BB dealer indicates that he intend to purchase USD one million at 1.1275.

At this stage the SB dealer knew that BB wanted to sell GBP otherwise he would have transposed the quote as 85/75 for base currency.
There is an element of trust, honesty and confidence among the dealers without any written rules and regulations. What is said by the dealer, he stands by it? However if a wrong quoted is given by mistake, a chance is given to the dealer to reconsider.

Deal is confirmed with delivery date after two working days.
A deal ticket would be generated by the system at both ends, containing more or less the following details;

- Deal Number (practice vary as per policy)
- Deal date
- Type of deal (spot, forward)
- Deal currency
- Rate of exchange
- Counter currency
- Counter party
- Value date
- Payment instruction
- Direction of deal (bought or sold)

Author used a customized application called "DealerMan". There are numerous products available for this purpose in the market. Deal will be forwarded through the system to the back office for inspection and approval and processed through the system to General Ledger and General Ledger Abstract and for recording in other subsidiary books.

Information about accounting system and processing is beyond the scope of this book.

SWIFT messages shall be prepared and authorized for transmission involving two to three authorized officers. These messages are meant for authorization of payment and receipt (Dr/ Cr) in the account with correspondent bank.

"SWIFT" stands for "Society for Worldwide International Financial Telecommunications". It is computer based a satellite communication network. Founded by Banks from all over the world and based in Brussels, Belgium. It links banks and brokers in every financial centre. It provides 24 hours services for secured send/receives interbank financial information. SWIFT allow member institution to send and receive financial information quickly and securely. SWIFT works through Relationship Management Application (RMA). Every member is issued a code (BIC) that contains abbreviation for Bank followed by Country City of Head office in alphabet and branch by number. Message type (MT) is numbered. SWIFT adopted the three letter abbreviation code for each currency created by International Organization for Standardization (ISO).

Information about SWIFT is beyond the scope of this book. The whole discussion is recorded by the system at both ends for reference and auditing. The transaction is closed in just half of a minute time.

FORWARD CONTRACTs

Since forward rates are determined by the discount and premium of the contracting currency, therefore the banker will assume the customer shall take up the delivery at a time most unfavorable to the bank; hence, if the currency is trade at a discount in the forward market, the bank will give minimum discount. On other hand if the foreign currency is quoted at a premium bank shall charge the maximum premium. Majority of option dated contracts cover a period of 31 calendar days or less. Longer period contract are less frequent. Following may be kept in mind dealing in option dated contracts;

- Both dates of option must be working dates.
- A threshold of delivery will be required.
- Notice period may be required for large delivery.

Suppose an **Importer** asks his bank in UK that he would require USD payment in three months time and needs to enter into a three month forward purchase contract for USD against GBP. Bank quotes the rate for three months as under;

Table 3.1

Currency: GBP/USD	Forward Rate Margins		
Spot Rate	One Month	Two Month	Three Month
1.1277 – 1.1287	30-25	55-40	95-75

The rates above indicate the indirect quotation and points/margin stated as High to low (Discount). It means that forward points shall be subtracted from the spot rate to obtain outright forward rate. As we know the customer needs USD to purchase in this contract and bank sells USD against GBP. Bank shall use the (Buy High Sell Low) technique. Bank shall give fewer dollars for each GBP. The base currency i.e. GBP is at discount and fewer USD will be given for each GBP, so USD is at premium in relation to GBP in the forward market. Forward points (highest) shall be **subtracted** from the buying (Bid 1.1277) price to further reduce the buying rate as under;

Table 3.2

Currency: GBP/USD	Forward Rate Margins		
Spot Rate	One Month	Two Month	Three Month
1.1277* – 1.1287	30-25	55-40	95-75
Margin to be deducted	30	55	95
Forward rate derived	1.1247	1.1222	1.1182*

- Three months outright forward rate for selling USD against GBP is 1.1182* USD per GBP.

A. Suppose the importer asks his Bank to quote the rate for three months forward selling USD or buying GBP with full option. Full option stands for any time within three months

Under this situation as the Bank will assume that the customer will use the option late until the last day of the option i.e. the last day of contract, therefore Bank shall deduct the maximum discount as above and this outright rate shall be quoted for three months with full option i.e. 1.1182* USD per GBP.

B. Suppose the Importer asks his Bank to quotes the rate for three months forward price with two month option. Two month option stands for option during the last two months of the contract. Under such a situation, Bank will assume that the customer will use the option late until the last day of the option i.e. the last day of contract, therefore Bank shall deduct the maximum discount as above and the same outright rate shall be quoted for three months with two month option i.e. 1.1182* USD per GBP.

C. Suppose the Importer asks his Bank to quotes the rate for three months forward price with one month option. One month option stands for option during the last one month of the contract. Under such a situation, Bank will still assume that the customer will use the option late until the last day of the option i.e. the last day of contract, therefore Bank shall again deduct the maximum discount and the same outright rate shall be quoted for three months with one month option i.e. 1.1182* USD per GBP.

Bank has quoted forward rates with all possible option but these are market rates. Bank shall arrange USD from the market for delivery to the customer on these competitive rates. No doubt bank shall provide services to the customer and support trade but not for free. Bank shall keep an element of income in the transaction for itself and therefore a spread may be included in the rate so quoted.

Conversely an **Exporter** can approach his bank for sale of his export proceeds. The option in these ways can be exercised by exporter. Bank view will change and assume in case of purchase of export proceed that customer shall exercise his option at the earliest of the option period as exemplified different scenarios as under;

Suppose an exporter approaches his bank in UK to sell USD to be received in three months time. Exporter enters into a three month forward sale contract of USD against GBP. Bank quotes the rate for three months as under;

Table 3.3

Currency: GBP/USD	Forward Rate Margins		
Spot Rate	One Month	Two Month	Three Month
1.1277 – 1.1287	30-25	55-40	95-75

In such a situation, Bank acts as the purchaser of foreign currency. Therefore the minimum margin i.e. 25/40/75 of each period shall be subtracted from the selling (Offer; 1.1287) price of GBP taking more USD for each GBP given as;

Table 3.4

Currency: GBP/USD	Forward Rate Margins		
Spot Rate	One Month	Two Month	Three Month
1.1277 – **1.1287***	30-25	55-40	95-75
Margin to be deducted	25	40	75
Forward rate derived	1.1262	1.1247	1.1212*

59

As we know foreign exchange rates are quoted by bank as a market maker and dealer, therefore rates are quoted with the perspective of a Bank/ Dealer. What the bank sells against base currency and what the bank buys against base currency. In this situation bank sells GBP against USD. Bank shall take more USD against GBP. The higher rate shall be applied (BL-SH)

Three months outright forward rate for buying USD against GBP is 1.1212* USD per GBP.

A.   Suppose the exporter asks his Bank to quotes the rate for three months forward buying USD or selling GBP with full option.

Under this situation, Bank will assume that the customer will use the option as early as the first day of the contract; therefore Bank shall quoted spot rate for three months offering no discount i.e. 1.1287* spot rate USD per GBP.

B.   Suppose the exporter asks his Bank to quotes the rate for three months forward sale price with two months option. Under this situation, Bank will assume that the customer will use the option as early as the first day of the option i.e. the first day of the second month; therefore Bank shall again deduct the maximum margin and that outright rate shall be quoted for three months with one month forward rate i.e. 1.1262*USD per GBP.

C.   Suppose the exporter asks his Bank to quotes the rate for three months forward sale price with one month option. Under this situation, Bank will assume that the customer will use the option as early as the first day of the option i.e. the first day of the third month; therefore Bank shall quote for three months with one month option i.e. 1.1247* USD per GBP.

Bank has quoted forward rates with all possible option but these are market rates. Bank shall arrange USD from the market for delivery to the customer on these competitive rates. No doubt bank shall provide services to the customer and support trade but not for free. Bank shall keep an element of income in the transaction for itself and therefore a spread may be deducted/ included as the case may be, to the rate so quoted.

FOREIGN EXCHANGE SWAP

Literal meaning of "SWAP" is an act of exchanging one thing for another. Foreign exchange swap is a simultaneous foreign currency purchase and sale but for different maturity dates. Foreign exchange swap is a combination of two deals; the purchase of a currency at spot and simultaneous sale of the <u>same currency</u> forward or sale of a currency spot and purchase of the <u>same currency</u> at future date. Foreign exchange swap is sale/purchase of a currency for two different dates to be completed in two different deals. Foreign exchange dealer arranges the FX swap as a single deal of two different value dates. Exchange of principal is executed at both the ends/legs. For example in a Euromarkets a client deposits USD with a bank for six month term. Another customer asks the bank for a loan of GBP for six months. Bank uses USD to purchase GBP spot and sell GBP six month forward against USD. Bank will earn interest on loan and pay the client the proceeds of forward sale as USD. The deposit by client is a separate contract. The loan to a client is also a separate contract independent of the sale purchase of currencies in question.

Foreign exchange swap is a pair of transactions of the same currency. It involves full exchange of principal amount at both dates unlike forward contract where actual deliveries are made at the future date. The sale and purchase are for the same amount of the same currency among the two and same counter parties. For example if a deal is for sale of USD one million spot against EURO, then purchase deal is also for USD one million against EURO at a specified and agreed upon future date. FX swap is the most widely traded instrument in foreign exchange market. There are three types of swap in the market;

SPOT AGAINST FORWARD SWAP

This is the simple and mostly used type of swap. In this type a spot sale/purchase of a currency against forward purchase/sale of a currency. One transaction is spot and the other is forward. On both dates actual exchange of principal amount takes place.

FORWARD AGAINST FORWARD SWAP

As evident from the title, this type of swap is forward against forward i.e. one transaction is executed three month in future and the other after that forward date i.e. after six month and referred to as 3x6.

SHORT PERIOD / BROKEN PERIOD SWAP

This type of swap is for a short period. The period may be as short as a day after spot value date and for a week, two or three.

FORWARD SWAP POINT'S QUOTATION

Like spot market and forward market, swap is also used by banks for speculation, Cash management, servicing clients and arbitrage (purchase of currency in one market and sale of the same currency in another market). The deal ticket contains almost the same detail with little variation referring to the nature and terms of transaction of transaction. Rates are quoted in dual way of Bid and Offer by the market maker but with forward points. It should be kept in mind that the rule of forward point quotation form apply herein is the same as; when forward margin quoted in the pattern of <u>low to high</u>, margin, is always meant to be <u>added</u> to spot rate to arrive at the outright forward rate as discount. Conversely when it is quoted in the pattern of <u>high to low</u> margin, it is always meant to be <u>subtracted</u> from spot rate as premium.

The same principle of premium and discount is applicable as discussed above in forward rate quotation. When forward margin is quoted in the Low to High pattern it added to the spot and when it is quoted from High to Low style, it is subtracted from spot. However, it is worth identifying as to which currency the market maker is dealing in i.e. which is Base and which is Counter currency. If base is being sold, rate is different and if Counter currency is being traded rate shall be different. For example;

Table 3.5

Currency	Spot Rate	Quotation Style
GBP/USD	1.1277 – 1.1287 Or 1.1277 – 10	
Forward Margin (pips)		
One Month	30-25	High to Low
Three Months	95-75	High to Low

In this situation if the market maker is selling/ purchasing the Base currency i.e. GBP against USD, he will add the forward margin to the selling/ purchasing rate of Base currency as the case may be. Identify the rate applicable to the nature of transaction. Conversely if he is buying or selling the Counter currency i.e. USD, he will add the margin to same whether purchasing or selling the Counter currency. Therefore the first step is identifying the applicable rate for the transaction. In case of High to Low quotation the margin shall be deducted. The rest of the applicability depends on the practice and rule of the transaction.

Table 3.6

Currency: GBP/USD	Forward Rate Margins		
Spot Rate	One Month	Two Month	Three Month
1.1277 – **1.1287***	30-25	55-40	95-75
Margin to be deducted	25	40	75
Forward rate derived	1.1262	1.1247	1.1212*

The Base currency GBP is being sold against USD. As such, the minimum margin i.e. 25/40/75 of each period shall be subtracted. Forward rates after deduction shall be for one month 1.1262(1.1287-0.0025) for two month 1.1247(1.1287-0.0040) and for three months 1.1212(1.1287-0.0075).

Since in FX swap there are two legs of the transaction i.e. Spot buy and forward sale or spot sale and forward buy therefore, it is an OTC transaction. This state of affairs makes the difference as to which rate to be quoted as Bid and which as Offer. Again there is difference in practice by the market in US and UK and rest of the world. However forward points are calculated in the same way mentioned already under the heading forward rates based on interest rate differential. Swaps are transacted for a period up to one year. Base currency amounts are identical at both ends of the deal.

USERS OF SWAP

Swap is not as popular with importer and exporter as popular is the outright forward purchase or sale. Swap is used by those who invest in foreign currencies or borrow in foreign currencies. Swap is used by banks where they are long in one currency and short in other and swap help them to reduce the risk. Banks manage their cash flow through foreign exchange swap. Speculators speculate on foreign exchange rate for investment and taking advantage of the market sentiments. Forward traders speculate on interest rate movement and as a result interest differentials and use FX swap for investment.

★ ★ ★ ★

Chapter Four

FOREIGN EXCHANGE DERIVATIVES

Derivative refer to a financial instrument, the value of which is based on an underlying security, like currency, commodity or stock index. Such Over the Counter (OTC) and derivatives traded on an organized exchange are used to manage risks and speculation.

CURRENCY SWAPS

Currency swap and Foreign exchange swap differ in that foreign exchange swap, wherein an interest rate differential between the two currency is taken into account in determining the forward rate for the forward delivery date, whereas in currency swap the interest differential is actually paid during the life of the swap agreement at each agreed payment dates. Currency swap is an over the counter agreement between two parties to swap interest rate payments on foreign currency loans. Currency swap is the most common method of hedging currency exposure in the long term financing facilities. It is an arrangement under which borrowers exchange the cash flows for both principal and interest amount. Under currency swap the two parties for two currencies with different interest rates of borrowing. The agreement process is somewhat as under;

First party is in one country or center and Second party is in another country or centre. First party is with its own currency and Second party is with its own currency. Principal is exchanged at agreed spot price on both date of contract- spot and future. The value in exchange of same currencies at the agreed spot rate shall remain the same. Interest amount is paid on each currency by respective parties on each agreed date over the life of the swap in accordance with terms of individual financing.

For example, a corporate entity in Canada has planned to purchase seven star hotels in New York. The entity needs 500 million USD to purchase the asset. If the entity approaches its bank in Canada for USD loan, Bank offers seven year loan at fixed rate 5% and Canadian dollar loan is offered at 6%.

Another multinational in USA has planned to establish an assembly in Canada. It needs 700 million CAD for the project. Bank in USA offers a seven year fixed rate loan for CAD at 8%, whereas loan in USD at fixed rate is available at 7%. The agreement for currency swaps en-shape as;

- Exchange of principal shall be made on the agreement date at agreed spot rate of exchange between USD/CAD1.4.
- Interest payment;
- Canadian entity shall pay interest on USD 500 million at 7% on each interest payment dates i.e. monthly, quarterly or bi-annually on the outstanding balance of loan for seven years.
- US entity shall pay interest on CAD700 million at 6% on each interest payment dates i.e. monthly, quarterly or bi-annually on the outstanding balance of loan for seven years.
- Exchange of principal amount shall be made at the maturity of loan after seven years at the spot of 1.4 as agreed at the outset of swap agreement and respective loans shall be adjusted.

First Leg at the time and date of Swap agreement; The Canadian entity shall buy USD 500 @ 1.4 from US entity and sell CAD 700 @ 1.4 to US Entity. Principal exchanged at this date of the agreement. Canadian entity shall pay interest @ 7% on USD dollar loan for seven years and US entity will pay interest on CAD @ 6%.

2nd Leg at the expiry date of swap agreement

Canadian entity shall buy USD 500 @ 1.4 from US entity and sell CAD 700 @ 1.4 to US Entity. Principal exchanged at this date of the agreement. Canadian entity shall pay interest @ 7% on USD dollar loan for seven years and US entity will pay interest on CAD @ 6%. The exchange of principal amount is reversed. Interest amount has already been settled. Principal is exchange to pay the loan amount at each respective bank in respective currency and in respective country.

CURRENCY FUTURES

Foreign Exchange market created forward contracts for protection against the risk of foreign exchange rates fluctuation. It provided the best way of protection with minimum possible cost to almost all the users. Future contract are like forward contract in that it is an agreement for the future delivery of the something (the "underlying") at an agreed price at the designated future period of time. However, there is an operational difference in both the contracts. It would not be out of place to indicate the difference at the outset for better understanding of its operational side.

FORWARD CONTRACTS VS FUTURE CONTRACTS

Forward contracts are traded over the counter (OTC) with no clearing house whereas future contracts are trade on the floors of exchanges with clearing house. Forward contracts are non-standardized in terms of amount and time period but future contracts are standardized in terms of amount and time period. Forward contracts are negotiated individually between buyer & seller identifiable. Future contracts are traded on the floor of an exchange by open outcry for bid/

offer without a need for identity the counter parties. Forward contracts have no secondary market. Future contracts have Exchanges and secondary market. For forward contract there is an acceptance and future delivery for completion. Future contracts are not supposed to be settled on future delivery only. In forward contract there is an acceptance and future delivery for completion. Future contracts are not supposed to be settled on future delivery only. There is no interim cash flow in forward contract; hence no valuation or mark to market during the period of currency of contract. Future contracts are marked to market and there is an interim cash flow; hence valuation & marked to market over the period of currency contract. There is no margin concept in forward contracts. Margin (Initial and maintenance) is retained and maintained with the Clearing House in case of futures. Forward contract holder is exposed to credit and/ or settlement risk. Future contract holder is least exposed to credit and/or settlement risk as holder is available with the exchange guarantees. The clearing house acts as a counter party to both sides of the trade. Any trader, broker, participant of FX market can enter into forward contract for any period. Only registered member of exchange can trade in futures business. Non member can trade through member brokers. No limit defined on the price fluctuation in the forward exchange market. There is a limit on price fluctuation of future contract. Price cannot appreciate/ depreciate beyond the limit set on the closing price of previous day. In forward contract business, banks retain the difference between buying and selling rate (spread) as income. In future contract there is a fixed rate commission of each contract bought and sold.

Currency Futures trading was introduced by Chicago Mercantile Exchange (CME) through the International Monetary Market (IMM), a division of CME in 1972. After the fall of fixed exchange rate and failure of Smithsonian system of exchange, all the major currencies were allowed to float freely on the basis of market forces i.e. supply and demand. The exchange rates were highly volatile and trade was fraught with exchange risk. The introduction of this specialized exchange was very happily received by trader and commercial users. It seemed that it was very much awaited. The purpose was to provide an alternate forum to those having true commercial needs for forward exchange contract with minimum risk. This kind of forum (exchange) was conceived by IMM as an extension of the commodity exchanges.

The positive response and success of IMM trading of Currency Futures, encouraged setting up of other exchanges in USA and other parts of the world, like New York Future Exchange (NYFE), Mid America Commodity Exchange (MAC), FINEX, the Financial Division of New York Cotton Exchange, Singapore International Monetary Exchange (SIMEX), London international Financial Future Exchange (LIFFE) etc. Futures market deals in currency future contracts. As evident from the definition above in a future contract the buyer agrees to take delivery of something at a specified price at the end of specified period of time and seller of the future contract agrees to deliver something at a specified price at the end of a specified period of time. Execution of the contract is achieved by accepting or delivering the specified currency on the value date of the contract. The term "buyer" or "seller" are used only connotative of the two parties to a future contract. Actually no buyer buys anything and no seller sell anything rather they commit themselves to a contract for delivering something in the future. Future contract are traded on the floor of an exchange and for each of the two legs of the contract there is clearing house as a counter party. Clearing house is seller for the buyer and clearing house is buyer for the seller. Future Currency contracts are standardize with defined contract sizes against USD in each currency traded on IMM in USA is available in five major currencies namely;

Table 4.1

Currencies	Contract Size against USD
GBP	62,500
AUD	100,000
CAD	100,000
EUR	125,000
JPY	12,500,000

Unlike forward exchange market wherein trading is done through communication systems on principal to principal basis knowing each other, at any given moment for any amount at a rate negotiable between commercial bank and their clients, the financial future market traders deal through authorized exchange members on the floor of an exchange for specific time during the working day and for specific threshold of contract size as stated above at a price (bid/offer) revealed on the screen at a central place. Time span of trade may vary at different exchanges geographically, but it is almost six to eight hours a day.

CURRENCY FUTURE OPERATION

Suppose that Mr. X has a credit balance of USD100, 000.00 in his account with Box Bank in USA on first January 20X2. Mr. X is of the opinion that GBP would appreciate relative to USD in future. He asks his banker who is member of IMM exchange to purchase GBP future contract for him which is quoted at GBP/USD 1.1277. Point to be noted that most of the exchanges quote futures currency prices in American terms i.e. as Indirect quotes means that a variable amount of USD against single unit of foreign currency.

INITIAL MARGINAL DEPOSIT

Margin is the distinctive feature of currency future contract. Since no exchange of principal and the underlying take place on the transaction date, margin is the binding element on the buyer and seller of the contract. On behalf of the client Box Bank purchased 20 contract of GBP (62,500) on first January due March (three months) at USD1.1277. On the contract date buyer and seller are required to deposit margin amount. When a position is taken by the investor for the first time (buyer & seller), a minimum dollar amount is deposited by the investors per contract as specified by the exchange. This amount is called Initial Margin. As the price of the future contract fluctuates each trading day the value of the deposit/ equity also changes. Equity in the account represents the total of margins deposited for all contracts purchased or sold for the first time on the exchange. All the daily gain or losses are posted to the margin account to calculate the net amount to be withdrawn (excess) of limit or deposited (deficient of limit) by the investor. As per rule of the exchange marginal deposit for GBP contract is USD5000 which comes to USD100, 000.00 (5000x20).

LEVERAGING OR GEARING

Margin deposits allow the investors to trade large notional amount of contracts. The investor need not to pay or deposit the entire amount of the contract. Mr. X the investor In our example can fund a position in the FX market equivalent to total amount of 20 contract i.e. GBP 1,250,000(62500x20). This facility enables the buyer and seller to earn profit or sustain a loss on the face value of contract(s), for commitment of a small amount of margin, depending on the movement of rate. Loss of seller is the profit of the buyer and vice versa. However, the degree of leverage available in the future market varies from contract to contract, as the initial margin requirement varies; the degree of leverage available varies accordingly. Further suppose that Mr. X rightly expected and GBP appreciated to USD1.1325 per GBP. Remember that maturity of contract is the third Wednesday of March. Mr. X has two options;

VARIATION MARGIN

He can wait until maturity and pocket the appreciation amount by withdrawing from the margin account (cash flow). Since Mr. X is buyer of the contract, there must be a seller (an Investor/ clearing house). Both the buyer and the seller must have opened margin deposit account with clearing house as per rules. When the rate appreciates the buyer earns as if he decides to dispose of the contract (selling it). He shall get higher price as compared to the one for which he purchased the contract. Clearing house calculate the position on daily basis. In the example USD 6000 (1,250,000 x (1.1325-1.1277), this amount of USD 6000 shall be debited to seller's margin deposit (loss) by the clearing house and through broker shall be paid to the buyer. The seller shall be asked to top up the margin account and deposit cash in case the margin deposit goes down the mandatory deposit limit. This is called Variation / Maintenance Margin. The variation margin deposit account of buyer and seller is adjusted on daily basis as a result of futures price fluctuation with closing rate of previous day. Point to note that if margin is not used up by the loss in exchange rate is repayable to the investors. However, commission as per rule shall be retained by the clearing house.

LIQUIDATION

Mr. X can actually sell the contract (offsetting) and earn profit. A party to a future contract has a choice to liquidate before settlement date and sell the contract. In this case the seller is not absolved of his commitment rather he is liable to deliver the contracted something (the "underlying") to the new buyer as per contract. Clearing house shall intimate the new buyer to the seller for delivery on due date on the same terms and conditions. On the settlement date i.e. third Wednesday of March, trading shall stop two working days before the third Wednesday of contract month and settlement take place. Financial future contracts have settlement dates on 3rd Wednesday in the months of March, June, September and December. On maturity date the buyer accepts the delivery of 20 GBP future contracts (GBP 1,250,000) and the seller liquidates his position by delivering the contract at the agreed upon price GBP/USD1.1277 receiving the value.

CURRENCY OPTION

Forward exchange contract is the one in which a currency can be bought or sold for delivery in future. Forward contract may stipulate delivery on a specific date i.e. June 30th which is called fixed dated forward contract, or during a specified period i.e. June 01–30 which is called option delivery forward contract. But in both situations the counter parties are obliged to fully settle the contract at the maturity date. Currency future contracts are designed for mitigating an exchange rate fluctuation risk. But currency futures are liquidated mostly by an offsetting sale or purchase rather than being settled through exchange delivery procedures. Both of the forms are designed around a forward commitment to exchange currencies at some future date. Forward contract entails a credit risk in case of default at the expiry date for many different reasons. Currency future contract entails the risk of non materialization of the order in terms of acceptable counter currency and desired period of time. Forward contract and currency futures both hedge an investor against the adverse and/ or favorable movement in FX rates. To do away with the shortcomings of both types of above contracts and to meet the requirement of the traders; importers/ exporters, the Philadelphia Stock Exchange created the world's first widely traded currency option in 1980. Foreign exchange option can be used to hedge against the risk of an adverse change in FX rates but at the same time if rate moves in favor of the investor, he can take advantage by utilizing the option. Under a currency option one of the dealing parties, the buyer (Holder), actually owns the rights to the contract and decides whether or not the contract is to be exercised/ settled. The buyer of the contract can let the currency option contract lapse without taking the delivery. On the other hand the seller (Writer) of the option has no flexibility in deciding whether or not the delivery shall take place. It means that holder/ buyer has full control of that decision. The word option relate to the delivery. Option means that buyer has the option of making or making delivery in a currency option delivery contract. Currency option is a contract between buyer (mostly client) and a seller (mostly bank) which gives the buyer the right, but not obligation (not obliged) to buy or sell a specified amount of currency at some time in future at a pre-determined exercise price/ strike price. The seller of the option gives the right to buyer for certain amount payable upfront called option price/ option premium. Buyer pays a premium to the seller for the option contract and the premium is retained (not refundable) by the seller irrespective of whether the buyer exercise the option or let it lapsed. The date after which the option become void is referred to as expiration date/ maturity date. Expiration date is usually Saturday before the 3rd Friday of the expiration month i.e. March, June, September and December. Options which are allowed to be exercised from the date of purchase/contract, at any time up to and including the expiration date is called an American style exercise/option. Such options style is used in USA market. Other style is European style in which option may be exercised only at the expiration date. However, settlement is allowed two working days as in vogue in FX market.

TYPES OF CURRENCY OPTIONS

CALL OPTIONS

A call option is an option to buy the underlying instrument. This type of option gives the buyer (Holder) the right to purchase or "call away" a specified amount of underlying foreign currency at a specified price up to a specified date. The price at which the foreign currency may be bought is the exercise price. The last date on which the option may be exercised is the expiration date or the maturity date. The price of the option is its premium.

PUT OPTIONS

A put option is an option to sell the underlying instrument. This type of option gives the buyer the right to sell or "put to" the issuer (Writer, the bank) of the option of a given amount of foreign currency at a given price on before a specific date.

FORMS OF CURRENCY OPTIONS

OVER THE COUNTER (OTC) OPTIONS

Banks and investment dealers are primarily the market makers in OTC options. It is the form usually written by an international bank to meet the particular requirement of its client. It is tailor made agreed between the counter parties in terms of amount and the expiry date serving their mutual interests. OTC is a dominant currency options market because of its liquidity and flexibility in terms of amount, currencies, expiry dates, strike price and minimum administrative cost related to margin requirements. The OTC daily turnover in currency options is far greater than the Exchange traded options. OTC currency option account for about 90% of the market.

CHARACTERISTICS OF OTC

- OTC option contracts take place between buyer and seller directly or through broker.
- OTC option contract are tailor made and flexible with respect to currencies, amount, expiry. The terms of the contract are freely negotiable between the counter parties.

• OTC requires no margin but premium.

International Currency Option Market Terms (ICOM Terms)

Due to the complex nature of option trading, a need was felt for a standardized common terminology. Owing to such need for avoid any confusion in trading options and legal documentation; British Banker Association (BBA) jointly with major Banks introduced London Interbank Currency Option Market (LICOM Terms). This was followed by US introducing USICOM Terms but finally in 1997 a common terminology was adopted as International Currency Option (ICOM). Hence trader while trading use the following common terms with harmonized meaning and connotations.

- ✓ Trade date
- ✓ Buyer & Seller
- ✓ Option Style (American or European)
- ✓ Option Type- Call or Put
- ✓ Call currency denomination & amount
- ✓ Put currency denomination & amount
- ✓ Strike Price
- ✓ Expiry date
- ✓ Expiry Time
- ✓ Expiry settlement date
- ✓ Premium Price
- ✓ Premium payment date
- ✓ Premium payment instructions

Suppose an importer in USA has contracted imports from UK. The payment of GBP to exporter is at deferred payment of three months. The importer is exposed to exchange risk. To hedge against the risk, the importer buys a call option of GBP contract GBP 32,500 at an agreed upon strike price of GBP/ USD 1.1277 from Box Bank. The importer would buy GBP from Box Bank against USD and pay to the UK exporter the GBP on the expiry date i.e. after three months. As per terms of option the importer is required to pay the option price i.e. Premium -say, USD 500. This non refundable premium is the reward for the Bank and cost for the importer. After three month the importer would pay USD 36,650 (32,500x1.1277). During this three month of contract, the exchange rate can fluctuate to the advantage of either party i.e. the importer or the bank.

Suppose, on the expiry/ delivery date USD lost its value and depreciated down to 1.3 per GBP;

Table 4.2

Contract Value	GBP 32,500
Strike Price	1.1277
Expiry	Three month from contract date
Value in GBP	32500X1.1277= USD 36,650
Option Premium	500
On the Expiry date	USD depreciated
Contract Value	GBP 32,500 (USD=36650+500= 37,150)
Strike Price	1.300
Value in GBP	32,500X1.300= USD 42,250
Net	42,250 – (36650+500) = USD 5,100

The importer is at advantageous position as spot market is higher than option bought by USD 5100. Importer would exercise the option. GBP is expensive in the spot market.

Suppose that USD appreciates to 1.03 spot rates, GBP depreciates; 32,500 x 1.03 = USD 33,475 33,475-(36,650+500) = USD (3,675), the importer is better to purchase from spot market and let the option lapse. Importer would save USD 3,675. Option becomes spot at the maturity date.

EXCHANGE TRADED OPTIONS

It is the form that is traded on a number of Exchanges like Philadelphia Stock exchange (PHLX) taken over by

NASDAQ since 2007 and known as NASDAQ OMX PHLX, The Index and Option Market (IOM) a division of Chicago Mercantile Exchange (CME) for option on IMM currency future contracts, Chicago Option Exchange (COE), London International Financial Future Exchange (LIFFE), etc. Like currency futures there are four settlement dates each year specified by each exchange. The underlying asset for currency option on an exchange can be a fixed amount of spot currency or it can be an equivalent currency future contract.

CHARACTERISTICS OF EXCHANGE TRADED OPTIONS

Most of the options traded on exchanges are in American style. There is a standardized instrument and standardized amount. There is a range of an "in the money"(ITM), "at the money"(ATM) or "out of the money"(OTM) strike prices in the Exchange. There is an expiry date. There is a margin payment.

Exchanged traded Currency Options at Philadelphia Stock exchange (PHLX) are offered against USD in seven major currencies i.e. GBP, AUD, CAD, EUR, CHF, NZD and JPY with contract size against USD as 62500, 10,000, 10,000, 10,000, 10,000, 10,000 and 1000,000 respectively. NASDAQ PHLX also allows customized option deals. It allow USD settled foreign currency options with negotiable exercise price, expiration date, exercise style with other features and benefit in line with commercial banks customized derivative products.

Exchanged traded Currency Option Contract at Chicago Mercantile Exchange (CME)- IOM are offered against USD in seven major currencies i.e. GBP, AUD, CAD, EUR,

NZD and JPY with contract size against USD as 62500, 100,000, 100,000, 125,000, 100,000, and 12,500,000 respectively.

Consider the other side of trade at an exchange and suppose that an Importer in USA has contracted imports from UK on 01 Jan 20X2. The payment of GBP100, 000 to exporter is at deferred payment of three months i.e. 31 March 20X2. The importer is exposed to exchange risk. To hedge against the risk, the importer have to buy GBP forward for payment at due date at the exchange. The spot rate GBP/USD 1.11277-1.1287. As mentioned earlier exchange offer standardized contracts. GBP contract size is 62500. Payment due is 100,000. First point is that total GBP contract required is 1.6 (100000/62500). It is equivalent to say 2 contract of total value of 125000. Second point to consider is the strike price. Three types of prices used in the exchange. Third point is the payment of premium. Premium is the cost of option for the importer and it is non refundable whatever the fate of option is in future whether let it lapsed or taken. Fourth point is to decide whether the importer will go for call option or put option. Call is to buy without obligation and put is to sell without obligation. Since importer is obliged to pay GBP, so he will buy Call option to hedge against the appreciation of GBP. Suppose;

Table 4.3

Investment Value	100,000
Exercise Price	1.14
Contract Size (GBP)	62,500
Number of Contracts	100,000/62,500=1.6, Say 2
Value of Contract	62500X2= 125,000
Exercise Price	125000 x1.14 =142,500
Call or Put	Purchase of Call option GBP
Premium	125,000X 0.16 = USD 20,000
USD appreciated on Expiry Date	From 1.11277- 1.1287 to 1.1160-1.1170
Market Spot deal	125,000X 1.1170 =139,625
Difference	142,500-139,625= 2875- expensive

The importer will let the option lapse and purchase GBP from market as the option contract value (142,500) is higher and importer has the right to let the option lapse and take from favorable market i.e. 139,625.

OTC & EXCHANGE TRADED OPTIONS COMPARED

Prices are less observable in OTC Options contract rather these are negotiated but in case of exchange traded contract prices are displayed and readily available in media and screens OTC option trade is executed through contact or through brokers whereas trading done in open arena through outcry on the floor in organised exchanges. Counter parties are known to each other in case of OTC option as the terms are negotiable. In exchange traded options parties are not known to each other but clearing house in the pivotal place. OTC Option ends in delivery in most of the trading. In exchange trade options few contracts result in delivery. Positions are not easy to offset or transfer in OTC trading. Options traded on the floor, position are easily offset or transferred. OTC in functional round the clock but it is not the case in exchange where limited trading hours are available. OTC is comparatively less regulated but exchange is well defined by rules and regulations.

PARTICIPANTS OF THE OPTIONS MARKET

Participants of Options market are the same as that of forward contracts and future currency traders. Option Market whether spot currency trading or forward contract/ future market is not different than spot sale purchase or forward contract for future delivery. Options provide the opportunity to take benefit of the favorable exchange rate.

INTERNATIONAL BANKS AND INVESTMENT DEALERS

A currency options in OTC are purchased from bank against the payment of premium. It is settled by exercising or selling it back to the bank/ writer. In the professional option market the Investment dealers use a wide range of options or combination of option to hedge their position or speculate on the exchange rates.

INTERNATIONAL TRADERS

Currency Options are particularly useful for importers and exporters. Importers need to make payment in foreign currency in future whereas exporters have receivables in foreign currency in future for import and export of goods and services respectively.

Chapter Five

FOREIGN EXCHANGE MANAGEMENT

History of foreign exchange and financial market tells many stories of financial risk faced overtime and devastated many financial institutions and even economies. Many examples can be quoted in this respect from financial mismanagement, financial crisis, and bank's failure to meet their obligations. The latest among these has been the financial crisis of 2006.

Central Banks and regulatory authorities must put in place stringent policies and procedures regarding risk management. The financial industry of the country must be made responsible to abide by those measures in their daily businesses and record keeping.

Foreign exchange risk management is a fundamental consideration and thought of as a complex, expensive and time consuming. Understanding and managing financial risk is of paramount importance for the successful running of foreign exchange and money market operation. Financial institution that trade in the financial market must formulate and implement a set of risk mitigation policies with proper authorization.

The recent past has witnessed very stern action by the legislators and regulators. A good chunk of resources have been earmarked by central banks and banks in their own capacity to better identify the financial risks and provide for its proper mitigation through different control systems. Financial risk may take different forms as mentioned hereunder;

RISKS INVOLVED IN FOREIGN EXCHANGE

Foreign exchange management is the process of minimizing the traders' exposure to foreign exchange rate fluctuation. Foreign exchange is central to international commerce. International traders need to convert its local currency into foreign currencies while making payment to the exporter and convert export proceeds into local currencies. When local currency appreciates relative to currencies of trading partners, due to strong local economy and stable political conditions, the import will get cheaper and export expensive. More imports shall increase the value of foreign currency and over time demand and supply shall bring balance in exchange rates.

EXCHANGE RATE RISK

Since spot market is highly volatile, sentiment and psychological factors play an important role in this market. Rumors may affect the spot rate within moments and rate may change to the disadvantage of a party to a transaction. On the other hand if an investor has assets denominated in foreign currency exposes him to uncertainty as to actual value of cash flow measured in book currency; say, USD. The actual amount of USD, the investor may receive depends on the exchange rate between the USD and the foreign currency. If the foreign currency depreciates in relation to USD (USD appreciates) the USD value of the assets shall be proportionally less and vice versa. If a bank in Switzerland, purchase USD for CHF 2 million at USD/CHF 1.005 which comes to USD 1,990,050 (2000000/1.005). Bank receives USD 1,990,050. After a week, the rate changes to USD/CHF 1.0015, bank would be able to purchase CHF 1,993,035, only thereby pocketing loss of CHF 6,965. Further if an investor has overbought a currency i.e. purchase is more than the sale the position is called "Long" and there is depreciation of that currency relative to the counter currency, a loss will result. Conversely if the investor has oversold a currency i.e. sale is more than the purchase the position is called "Short" and there is depreciation of that currency relative to the counter currency, gain will accrue. Therefore measures are necessary to taken to secure position.

INTEREST RATE RISK

Interest rate risk arises due to changes in interest rates in different centers and its effects on the currency of trade. For example borrowing in one currency, converting it into another currency that pays higher interest rate and reconverting in account currency carries the risk of exchange rate as well as interest rate. This adverse movement of currencies creates exchange loss. If a bank in Switzerland takes advantage of the high rate of interest in USA i.e. 4%, as compared to local rate as 3.75%. The bank converts CHF 2 million into USD/CHF 1.005 which comes to USD 1,990,050. The investment in three months Treasury bill at maturity gives USD 2,009,950 (1990050+ (1,990,050*.04*90/360)). During the three month period interest rate in Switzerland increased from 3.75% to 4.25%. This change in interest rate also changed the exchange rate between the respective currencies i.e. USD/CHF 0.9925. Bank would reconvert USD into CHF at 0.9925. Bank would receive CHF. 1,994,876. Bank has lost CHF 5,124, in the transaction. If the foreign currency depreciates in relation to USD (USD appreciates) the USD value of the assets shall be proportionally less and vice versa. Therefore measures are necessary to be taken to secure position.

CREDIT RISK

Credit risk is the risk that counter party would not meet his obligation at the time maturity/ due date. Banks lend money to many clients. The client may default on his repayment on due date. This default can be willful in some cases and may be commercial and genuine in others (bankruptcy).

Before entering into a deal, it is an established practice to have analyzed the counter party credit worthiness before and after on regular basis. The international credit rating agencies provide creditable opinion on parties besides internal valuation policies and procedures.

SETTLEMENT RISK

Foreign exchange spot deals are settled within two business days whereas forward deals are settled after a period of more than two working days and straddle over long period. Both kinds of deals involve future for both or at least one of the counterparty and future is always uncertain. Settlement risk is sustained in case where one party part with the payment before the payment by the counter party. This may not be intentional but due to differing time zone and clearing system processes involved. There is a chance of failure on the part of one leg to complete the transaction. If one party in one time zone pay today and the other party pay after two days, the first party carries the settlement risk due to reason beyond control of the party to the exchange contract.

POLITICAL AND LEGAL RISK

This kind of risk relate somewhat to settlement risk and credit risk. During the period of two business days in case of spot settlement and more seriously in case of forward settlement, the political and legal scenario may change and the investor is confronted with non receipt of contracted currency. The dealer is required to have the knowledge of the crucial political and legal changes expected in the framework of international trade. Restriction on foreign exchange by the government of the counter party can pose a serious issue with grave consequences.

MANAGING THE RISKS

Foreign exchange business like any other business is not free from risks. Risk that part of future which can be quantified into probability of outcome whereas uncertainty is a situation in future which is not quantifiable. Investors and Traders attempt to minimize the risk through various steps taken in this regards. Since Banks, Investment dealers, corporate participants and authorized dealers in foreign exchange are licensed and authorized by the regulators like Central Bank and Securities Exchange Commission; they are also subjected to rule and regulations so devised by the regulators and individual governing bodies i.e. Board of Directors (BoD) and Management Committees. Branches and sub offices are assigned with limit of foreign exchange business and exposure limits. These limits are strictly observed by the business. Daily and periodic MIS are submitted to the controlling offices for review. Variances and violations are addressed. Periodic reports are also submitted to the regulators for review. Compliance is ensured at all levels to avoid any untoward situation and eventuality. Penalties are imposed by the regulators for violations and strict adherence to rules and regulations is required.

EXCHANGE RATE RISK & INTEREST RATE RISK

Since spot market is highly volatile, sentiment and psychological factors play an important role in this market. Due to volatility in foreign exchange rates, foreign exchange risk has become a key challenge for the treasury of an international participant. International trade of goods and services or investment in either local or foreign currency, the trader is required to monitor the exchange rates.

Foreign exchange exposure limit
Foreign Exchange position limit

Trader manages risk for profit. High risk entails high profit. But profits are not guaranteed, however not earning profit is also a risk of opportunity loss. The amount that could be lost by assuming a particular level of risk must also be taken into account. Within a branch office a trader/dealer transact business in the market but it is not unlimited because unlimited business may end in unlimited loss. Therefore limit is assigned to a dealer based on his experience and performance (Dealer's limit). Limit may be established for the net long or short position for a given day. Limit are imposed on each currency(Currency limit) traded by the dealer and even for the term like maximum long and short position in one month area may be different than it is in the one year or more. Limits are also imposed on uses of foreign currency by the public for consumption like education, medical facility etc. These limits may be determined for a branch by the Head Office or controlling office and for a bank or an investment dealer by the regulator.

Overnight exposure limit are assigned to dealer for long and short position in each currency on an overnight basis (Foreign exchange exposure limit). Each authorized dealer is given an open position limit in foreign exchange taking into account its business volume. The limits are intended to cover the position of branches of a bank including balances in account with correspondent banks. Authorized dealers are directed to avoid becoming overbought or oversold in foreign currencies in spot as well as forward contracts.

To ascertain compliance of the limit so determined by the regulators, reports of Foreign Exchange Exposure limit are submitted periodically to the controlling offices and to the regulator through the controlling offices.

CASH MANAGEMENT

Cash management in the context of foreign exchange operation consist of monitoring the balances in Nostro (our account with you) account with overseas branches and correspondents, on daily basis, to;

- Avoid loss on large idle balances in account
- Avoid cost on unplanned overdraft.
- Avoid loss of reputation in case of failure to meet our liabilities for insufficient balance.

Therefore, it is important that trader keep an accurate track of foreign currency balances in Nostro account. This shall be achieved through daily maintenance of Cash Position in each currency and for each bank showing the opening balances from the mirror account in book of our Nostros account held abroad. Dealers know the major currencies of trade and their account maintenance with correspondent banks. All the transactions in those currencies are routed through these Nostros on day to day basis. Reconciliation of account is performed on daily basis to avoid any transaction missed or delayed. Correspondent banks, on our standing instructions provide daily Statement of account (SOA) to update and reconcile our record in the mirror account. This activity of updating and reconciliation provide the opportunity to use the extra fund available in the account or replenish the account in case of insufficient balance and maintain square position as per assigned limits.

GAP ANALYSIS

Banks in particular, raise funds (liabilities) from its clients in various accounts with different maturities. Demand deposit is free money used by banks for earning but it can be claimed by depositors any time in banking hours through cash or transfer. Time deposit with different maturities, are used by bank for investment (assets) of different maturities, but it is not free money and there may be a notice or call requirements. Investment of short term liabilities in creating long term assets cause loss due to immediate costly cover up from market in case of claims presented for payment. Conversely raising short term assets with funds of long term is also not a prudent business strategy as long term liabilities are costly whereas short term asset fetch little income. Gap management consists of keeping a track of and making good in time any mismatch between assets and liabilities. Such gap may expose bank to the risk of adverse interest rates cost or risk of cash shortages in times of claim of withdrawal. It becomes very costly and difficult to fund at short notice. It can lead to liquidity crunch and may tell on the reputation of the bank. Monitoring and control is achieved through maintenance of GAP Analysis Sheet for each currency. These system sheets are maintained from present and projecting into future, showing for each future date or period the inflows and outflows, the net of the flows for each date or period and the net cumulative position. The fund manager is able to keep within the prescribed gap limit and to take corrective measure appropriate to the indication well in time. Interest rate risk arises due change in interest in different centers and its effect on the currency of trade and balance in accounts. For example borrowing in one currency, converting it into another currency that pays high interest rate and reconverting in account currency carries the risk of exchange rate as well as interest rate risk. This adverse movement of currencies creates exchange loss.

COVERAGE OF CREDIT RISK AND SETTLEMENT RISK

Before entering the deal, it is an established practice to have analyzed the counter party credit worthiness before and after on regular basis. Approved AML rules and regulations, KYC and CDD procedures and practices are exchanged with the counter parties. The international credit rating agencies also provide credible opinion on parties. After analysis of credit worthiness an exposure limit is assigned based on the credit score card to the counter party subject to the criteria defined by controlling office and /or regulator. Per party exposure and per bank exposure limits are maintained. Party wise record of outstanding contract is maintained and regularly updated to ensure that no exposure beyond limit is taken. Such limit shall help guard against default in case of loans and settlement in case of foreign exchange exposure taken on counter parties.

COVERAGE OF POLITICAL AND LEGAL RISK

This kind of risk relate somewhat to settlement risk and credit risk. During the period of two business days in case of spot settlement and more seriously in case of forward settlement, the political and legal scenario may change and the investor is confronted with non receipt of contracted currency. The dealer is required to have knowledge of the crucial political and legal changes expected in the framework of international trade particularly and in the economy in general. Restriction on foreign exchange by the government of the counter party can pose a serious issue with grave consequences. There are agencies like Moody's, Fitch, D&B, S&P etc reporting on the credit worthiness of corporation as well as reports on the economy of sovereign state.

FX TERMINOLOGIES

Agent: One who agrees to act in accordance with the terms of a mandate on behalf of another, his principal; banks act as agents for other banks in a variety of ways; the services curried out largely depend upon the agency agreement existing between the banks in question.
Appreciation: An increase in foreign exchange value of a currency when exchange rates are flexible.
Arbitrage: The switching of funds from one financial market to another to take advantage of higher yield or capital gain opportunities as result of interest or exchange rate differentials prevailing between two or more centers.
ARR: Alternate Reference Rate; After the disclosure of rate manipulation of LIBOR in 2012, The US Fed constituted a ARR Committee to find robust replacement for gradual phasing out of LIBOR. The committee came up with Secured Overnight Financial Rate (SOFR) base on the rate paid by Financial Institutions to each other to borrow cash overnight in transactions collateralized by US Treasury securities. Since these are observable (Level 1- Fair value) transaction, hence considered less prone to manipulation as compared to LIBOR. By June 2023 LIBOR will be discarded. N.Y Fed publishes the latest SOFR on its web site each business day at 8.00 am for one to 12 months.
Ask rate: The price at which a bank or a broker is willing to sell.
At-the Money: Strike/Exercise price of an option that equal the current spot price are referred At-the- Money (ATM).
Basis point: Fourth decimal place (.0001) is called point and fifth decimal point (.00001) is called "pip" in exchange rate quotation.
Bear: Speculator who expects a currency to become weaker and sells that currency forward expecting to make a profit an exchange.
Beneficiary: Payee or recipient, usually of money. Party in whose favor a credit is established; in the majority of credits issued the beneficiary is an exporter of goods.
Bid Rate: The lower side of interest rate quotations; it is the rate of interest a bank is prepared to pay for deposits or to acquire securities.
Broker: One who brings together dealers who are buyers and dealers who are sellers of foreign currency, charging a brokerage for the service.
Broker (insurance): One who arranges a contract of insurance between an
under-writer and an insured; a broker is not a party to the contract but merely acts as an agent for the insured; it follows that a good broker should obtain for his client the best cover and terms available by approaching a wide variety of insurers.
Bull: Speculator who expects a currency to become firmer and buys that currency forward expecting to make a profit.
Call: Right to demand repayment of debt. Redeem outstanding loan stock. Option, to purchase securities /currencies at an agreed price and during a specified period.
Call Account: Deposit account, usually interest bearing, from which funds may be withdrawn " at call" (on notice being given).
Capital: Equity or shares plus profit retained plus loan and debenture stock.
Cross Rate: The direct relationship between two non-indigenous currencies of the centre concerned with the transaction; for example, all non-sterling exchange rate for deals done in the UK are cross rate - e.g. $/DM and US $ Can $.
Contract of sales: Bargain concluded between buyer and seller; the contract may be arranged by word of mouth informally, or may be the subject of a detailed sales agreement in writing and signed formally.
Correspondent Bank: Agent bank to which the principal bank communicates instructions for action.
Cost of fund: Terms sometimes used as the basis for a loan pricing particularly when the source of funding is uncertain or includes reserve assets what is meant by this term should be established if it is to be of any practical value; it should be noted that the normal funding

cost of a commercial loan is the offered rate, being the rate which the bank has to pay to another bank in the market for the funds obtained for the purpose.
Cross rate (exchange): An exchange rate between two currencies neither of which is US dollar.
Cross forwards: A forward exchange contract between two currencies neither of which is US dollar.
Currency: Usually implies foreign money rather than money in general.
Credit Rating: An assessment of the degree of creditworthiness of an organization; used to determine whether a beneficiary credit status is sufficient for the advising bank to accept the beneficiary's own indemnity for discrepancies on documents presented under a credit.
Certificate of Deposit: Interest bearing negotiable bearer certificate which evidences a time deposit with the bank. D/A Instructions for the commercial documents to be released to the drawee on acceptance of the bill of exchange.
Dealer: One authorized by his bank to deal on the foreign exchange market.
Deposits: Demand Liabilities of a bank in the form of current account funds or time liabilities like monies at a call, notice or fixed term, local or foreign currency.
Depreciation: A decrease in foreign exchange value of a currency when exchange rates are flexible.
Derivative: A financial asset such as a futures or options contract, the value of which is derived from the claim it makes against some underlying asset, such as a foreign currency.
Discount: The forward margin of a currency that is less expensive forward than the spot rate; the discount is added to the spot rate to which it relates.
Discount (FX): Forward margin of a currency that is less expensive than the spot rate.
Euro-currency: Bank deposits recorded in the name of a non resident of the country of the currency lodged.
Forward contract: Deal where the exchange is to be more than two working days from the date of the deal.
Forward-forward Contract: Forward sale against further forward purchase or forward purchase against further forward sale.
Covering/Funding: Acquisition of liabilities to match cover or balance the particular asset or assets for which they are acquired.
Exposure: A commonly used abbreviation for FX exposure.
Firm currency: A currency expensive in terms of other currencies.
Fibor: France interbank Offered rate.
Funds: Money in any currency, unless specifically stated.
Gearing: There are several formulae used, so the basis of a gearing ratio should always be established to be meaningful by ensuring comparison of like with like; a commonly used formula is; Total liabilities (footings) less capital base divided by capital base.
Hedge/ cover: Action taken to isolate assets, liabilities or income stream from the consequences of changes in exchange rates.
Hibor: Hong Kong interbank Offered rate.
In-the Money: Exercise price of an option that is superior to the current spot price are referred In-the Money (ITM).
Intrinsic Value: Value of the currency option that is "in- the- money (ITM)"
Leverage: Degree of exposure of securities to market risks; the capital structure of a company may be increased by issues of loan stock as well as equity, and the risks relationship between the two may be described as the leverage.
LIBOR: London interbank offered rate; the rate upon which loans are frequently determined; LIBOR will vary according to market conditions and will of course depend upon the loans period as well as the currency in question; it may be found that at the same time, for the same currency and for the same period, the quotation of a LIBOR figure by one bank in London and another in London will differ slightly; this would be expected if one bank were already long of the currency for that period, having just taken in a matched deposits, and the other bank position were different.

Liquidity: Ability to service debt and redeem or re-schedule liabilities at maturity and the ability to exchange other assets for cash.

Listing: Obtaining a quotation on a stock market for loan stock or equity which may then be traded on the stock exchange.

Local currency: Usually employed in the context of the indigenous legal tender (money) of the country of payment; the local currency of Pakistan is 'rupee' and US is dollar.

Long: Excess of purchases over sales is called long.

LORO: "Loro" a Latin word mean their- third party account with correspondent bank.

Margin: Difference between the spot and forward prices of a currency; if the forward price of the currency is greater than the spot price the margin is said to be 'at premium'; if the forward valve of the currency is less than the spot.

Maturity: Dates on which a loan, bill or other debt instrument falls due for repayment. Due date of payment of a term bill or note.

Miss-matched maturity: When the maturities of the funding cover and the loan or other asset do not coincide.

Mirror Account: Account Maintained by a bank in its books, of their correspondent accounts as mirror of affording transactions in the mirror account exactly the same way as effected by correspondent bank in the account of bank.

Negotiation: 1. Purchase of an outward collection, thereby providing finance by the exporter. 2. "Doing a deal" "treating", "bargaining", "settling terms". 3. Purchase under a confirmed credit (without recourse to beneficiary) or under an unconfirmed credit (with recourse to the beneficiary) of drafts which under the credit terms the issuing bank has undertaken to pay. 4. A form of ' payment ' of a credit by a bank other than the advising bank; this may be the beneficiary's bank which would claim reimbursement from the issuing bank directly, crediting the beneficiary. New York prime: The US banks' equivalent of the UK base rate; it is not a market rate as such but forms the rating basis for some short- term commercial loans; the rate are not altered on a daily basis for practical loan administration reasons; however , when the trend of the cost of the underlying funds changes ,NYPLR will be moved into line; loan may be based on fixed or on floating prime rates; the majority are based on the latter so that the loan will fluctuate broadly in line with the market conditions; loans that are based on fixed prime will run of the prime rate ruling at the time of funds are drawn down, and as such must be considered as any other fixed interest lending.

Nostro: "Nostro" derived from a Latin word "noster" represents our account. It refers to our account with correspondent bank. It may be with one's own branch or with other bank.

Offer: Price over which a loan may be based or a security purchased from the market or a bill discounted.

Open position: The long (above) or short (below) position at any time on which an exchange risk is run.

Option: The customer's right to deliver or to take delivery of a specified sum in foreign currency at any time or times during an agreed period.

Out-of the- Money: Exercise price of an option that is inferior to the current spot price are referred At-the Money (OTM).

Premium: Forward margin of a current i.e. more expensive powered then the spot rate; the premium is deducted from the spot rate to which it relates.

Put: Option to sell securities/ currency at a determined price and during a specified period.

Rate of Exchange: The price or value of a unit of one currency in terms of another.

Rating: Assessment of the quality of an issue by an established rating agency.

Secondary market: Market in which securities are traded after issue when the initial distribution has finished.

Short: Excess of sales over purchases.

SIBOR: Singapore interbank Offered rate.

Spot: The exchange rate is fixed immediately for delivery of the currency two working days from the date of the deal.

Spot against forward position: Extent to which spot currency holdings are married against forward sales; Found by subtracting forward purchase from forward sales.

Spot against forward transaction: A transaction in which a purchase or sale of spot currency is made against a corresponding sale or purchase of the same currency forward.

Spot next: Simultaneous selling of currency for delivery at spot and buying it back for delivery the day after, and vice versa.

Spread: Difference between the dealer's buying and selling, borrowing and lending, rates.

Swap: A spot purchase against a forward sale or a spot sale against a forward purchase.

Swift: Society for World Wide Inter-Bank Financial Tele- Communication.

Tom-next: Simultaneous selling of a currency for delivery tomorrow and repurchase on the spot delivery date (the following day or vice versa.

Units of account: Composite currency units designed to reduce exchange exposures of both borrower and investor.

Value date: Date on which funds are actually available for use by the bank in its Nostro account abroad, being the date agreed for settlement of a foreign currency transaction.

Vostro: "Vostro" derived from a Latin word "voster" represents our account. It refers to your account with us as respondent bank.

Weak currency: A currency may be described as weak when it is potentially cheaper in terms of other currencies.

About The Author

Nadir Khan

On receiving master's degree in Business Administration, he joined premier international bank with having presence in all leading international financial markets. He worked in different roles in domestic as well as in international banking for thirty-five years. He gathered hands-on exposure and experience in foreign exchange trading, conventional and Islamic-based money market business, conventional and Islamic-based security market trading, conventional and Islamic-based advances and syndication, and international trade for almost a decade, as Manager & General Manager, Offshore Banking Unit (OBU) in a tax-heaven market in the Middle East. During the service, he also received professional certificates in conventional banking, Islamic banking, and accountancy. The author had the opportunity to partner business with world-class giant banks and financial institutions. As a teacher, the author taught bankers the subject of foreign exchange & credit, for six years as an in-house faculty member.

Since the global marketplace is fast changing owing to the use of computers & internet; traders, managers, and foreign exchange professionals need to enhance their foreign exchange know-how for better performance in their professional roles. To this end, foreign exchange basics, operations, and management are presented in the book "Understanding Foreign Exchange".

References

- Principles of Money, Banking and Financial Markets, 8E, Lawrence S. Ritter & William L Silber- ISBN 0-465-06367-5.

- An introduction to Foreign Exchange & Money Markets: The Reuter Financial Training Series- ISBN 0-471-83128-X.

- Foreign Exchange Handbook; Managing Risks & opportunity in Global Currency Markets; Paul Bishop & Don Dixon- ISBN 0-07-005474-6.

- Foundation of Financial Markets and Institutions; International Edition Frank J. Fabozzi, Franco Modigliani, Michael G. Ferri- ISBN 0-13-176827-1.

- Foreign Exchange and Money Market Operations; Swiss Bank Corporation

- International Finance; 5E, Maurice D. Levi

- Investment Appraisal and Financial Decisions; Steve Lumby ISBN 0-412-58840- 4.

- Finance of Foreign Trade and Foreign Exchange 6E, Dr. Asrar H. Siddiqi; ISBN 978-969-407-455-9.

www.ingramcontent.com/pod-product-compliance
Lightning Source LLC
Chambersburg PA
CBHW071129240526
45465CB00024B/1549